WALKING THE ITALIAN LAKES

by Gillian Price

2 POLICE SQUARE, MILNTHORPE, CUMBRIA LA7 7PY
www.cicerone.co.uk

© Gillian Price
First edition 2012
ISBN: 978 1 85284 657 2
Printed by KHL Printing, Singapore.
A catalogue record for this book is available from the British Library.
Maps by Nicola Regine.
All photographs are by the author unless otherwise stated.

Dedication

To dear Nicola, my special sherpa

Acknowledgements

Firstly a great big 'thank you' to Jonathan Williams of Cicerone for suggesting we explore these breathtaking lakes! We had no idea they were so beautiful.

I'd like to acknowledge helpful suggestions from Gillian Arthur, Roberto Ricca of Bresciatourism and Mathilde Zuijdwegt of IAT Menaggio, as well as the enthusiastic Tourist Office staff of Bellagio, Cannero Riviera, Cannobio, Como, Gravedona, Iseo, Limone, Lovere, Luino, Riva del Garda, Torri del Benaco, Stresa, Verbania and Malcesine.

Big brother Marty made good use of his running shoes checking out alternate routes, and his taste buds, in the quest for that perfect evening meal.

Advice to Readers

While every effort is made by our authors to ensure the accuracy of guidebooks as they go to print, changes can occur during the lifetime of an edition. If we know of any, there will be an Updates tab on this book's page on the Cicerone website (www.cicerone.co.uk), so please check before planning your trip. We also advise that you check information about such things as transport, accommodation and shops locally. Even rights of way can be altered over time. We are always grateful for information about any discrepancies between a guidebook and the facts on the ground, sent by email to info@cicerone.co.uk or by post to Cicerone, 2 Police Square, Milnthorpe LA7 7PY, United Kingdom.

Front cover: The pretty village of Campino overlooks central Lago Maggiore (Walk 2)

CONTENTS

Map key

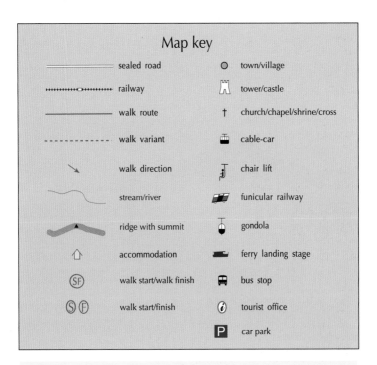

—————— sealed road	○ town/village
++++++○++++++ railway	🏰 tower/castle
—————— walk route	† church/chapel/shrine/cross
– – – – – walk variant	🚠 cable-car
↘ walk direction	chair lift
〜〜 stream/river	funicular railway
ridge with summit	gondola
⌂ accommodation	ferry landing stage
(SF) walk start/walk finish	🚌 bus stop
(S) (F) walk start/finish	(i) tourist office
	P car park

Warning

Mountain walking can be a dangerous activity carrying a risk of personal injury or death. It should be undertaken only by those with a full understanding of the risks and with the training and experience to evaluate them. While every care and effort has been taken in the preparation of this guide, the user should be aware that conditions can be highly variable and can change quickly, materially affecting the seriousness of a mountain walk. Therefore, except for any liability which cannot be excluded by law, neither Cicerone nor the author accept liability for damage of any nature (including damage to property, personal injury or death) arising directly or indirectly from the information in this book.

To call out the Mountain Rescue, ring 118: this will connect you via any available network. Once connected to the operator, ask for *Soccorso Alpino*.

Monte Zeda dominates the western branch of Val Cannobina (Walk 9)

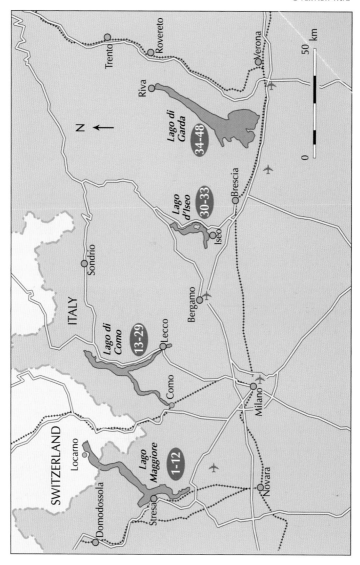

Approaching San Martino the path has a wonderful outlook on the lake (Walk 14)

INTRODUCTION

Nothing in the world could compare to the charms of these days spent on the Milanese lakes.
Stendhal (1783–1842)

A clutch of magnificent lakes spreads over the north of Italy at the foot of the gigantic Alpine chain on the border with Switzerland. Hemmed in by awesome cliffs, the glittering expanses of Maggiore, Como, Iseo and Garda have been visited by English-speaking holidaymakers since the days of the Grand Tour for their exquisite villas and lush gardens where camellias and rhododendrons spill over terraces.

Nowadays the great Italian lakes are well-known destinations for holidaymakers from the four corners of the globe, attracted by relaxing ferry cruises, romantic waterfront restaurants, picturesque villages, verdant alpine landscapes and dramatic views. A small percentage of visitors is drawn to the area for its outdoor activities, mainly the excitement of windsurfing and sailing. Yet just a few steps beyond the popular lakefronts a wonderful world of footpaths waits to be discovered by enthusiasts of all levels of experience and ability, from a leisurely waterfront stroll to a demanding 5-hour hike to the heights of alpine mountains. Well-marked straightforward routes can be enjoyed on short or longer walks, easily fitted into the space of a day. And every one

of them can be accessed by the excellent local public transport network, be that ferry, train, bus, cable car, chair lift or funicular. The walking around these beautiful lakes makes use of a system of age-old paved mule tracks once used to link remote hamlets and cross the Alps in the interests of trade, pilgrimage and travel. There are also lakeside promenades as well as clear paths through woods and mountain valleys.

The four lakes are quite distinct in flavour and atmosphere – and all strikingly beautiful – so how do you decide which one to start with? To caricature each one briefly, laid-back Maggiore boasts a bevy of picturesque islands-cum-villages that vie with quintessentially romantic Como for elegance in terms of villas and gardens. Garda is somewhat more dramatic and alpine in flavour with awesome cliffs around the upper lake, while little brother Iseo is petite and more remote than the other three. Rest assured that once your enthusiasm is fired you'll want to see them all!

The four lakes owe their formation to the huge glaciers that slowly spread down from the Alps towards the plains hundreds of thousands of

Beyond Bellano is the Dervio peninsula in upper Lago di Como (Walk 22)

years ago, scooping out giant channels. The glaciers carried with them rock debris which they bulldozed into long uniform ridges, known as moraines. When temperatures rose – around 12,000 years ago – the ice began to melt and retreat, leaving elongated troughs which filled with water to form spectacular lakes. Lying on a north–south axis, they resemble

THE LINEA CADORNA

In the period preceding World War I, the fledgling Republic of Italy feared an invasion from Germany and Austria by way of neutral Switzerland, and set on the idea of protecting its frontiers. The Linea Cadorna, named after its principal creator General Luigi Cadorna, became reality between 1912 and 1916. An incredible 40,000 men were put to work constructing a man-made barrier stretching across the mountain tops and valleys of the alpine foothills up to the 2000m mark from Passo del Sempione northwest of Lago Maggiore all the way to Chiavenna well north of Lago di Como, and touching on the shores of the great lakes themselves. They constructed 296km of roads, 398km of mule tracks and 72km of trenches, as well as lookout posts, command structures and barracks (never thankfully put to the test), still in remarkably good condition. Sections of the Linea Cadorna are visited on Walks 3, 7 and 8 on Lago Maggiore, as well as Walk 16 on Lago di Como.

deep fjords, wedged between line after breathtaking line of rugged mountain ridges rising well over 2000m. Fed by rivers and streams running straight off the Alps, it takes until midsummer for their crystal-clear waters to reach around 24°C – a bearable temperature for swimming.

For information about the distinctive culture of each lake, see the individual chapter introductions.

PLANTS AND FLOWERS

The Italian lakes offer much for flower lovers to admire as the equable climate and a broad altitude range guarantee myriad Mediterranean as well as alpine species. The spontaneous displays of wildflowers complement the magnificent and exotic plants found in the many formal villa gardens.

Exquisite wildflowers can be expected as early as April and May (spring) at lower altitudes, while the main display on the high alpine mountain ridges gets underway in June. Blooms and colours continue through to late summer (August–September), while autumn (October) brings russet hues in woods and forests. Highlights include the gorgeous peonies in the 'Botanical Garden of Europe' – namely Monte Baldo on Lago di Garda – brilliant orange lilies in shady meadows, the concentrated blue-purple hue of the willow-leaved gentian that blooms in gay clumps on open grassland, and a precious array of true alpine species, such as cinquefoil and alpine cornflower. Orchids are always a delight, and one special treasure is the rare insect orchid named after Lago di Garda (though not exclusive to that area): *Ophrys Benacensis*. An

The beautiful grounds of Villa Melzi, Lago di Como (Walk 24)

13

attractive and commonly encountered flowering bush is the smoke tree, its fluffy orange blooms reminiscent of clouds of smoke.

High stone walls are often adorned with magnificent bouquets of straggling caper plants, their open white petals brandishing purple pistils. It is their buds, picked and pickled or salted, which are the familiar ingredients of Italian cuisine. Grape vines flourish in the mild climate as do olives, especially along the sun-blessed lake shores of Lago di Garda.

WILDLIFE

One presence, albeit mysterious, that sets Lago di Como aside from the other northern lakes is the 'dreaded' Lariosaurus, a mythical reptilian creature said to resemble the famed Loch Ness monster in appearance and behaviour. However Larrie (as it has been nicknamed) is reputedly smaller – under 2m in length – but much more ferocious than its Scottish counterpart!

Walkers in woods will often notice hoof marks in the mud and scratchings

(Clockwise from top left) Brilliant orange lily; delicate caper blooms; willow-leaved gentians; peonies on Monte Baldo

Olives flourish in the warm climate

and diggings in the undergrowth, a sure sign of the presence of wild boar. Actual sightings are extremely rare as the creatures are very timid.

Chances are better of spotting roe deer flitting between trees, while higher rocky terrain is home to the dainty goat-like chamois, recognisable for their trademark crochet-hook horns and dark patched rear quarters. Grassland over the 800m mark is home to colonies of endearing alpine marmots, often seen dashing across

A marmot at its burrow

the meadows on a quest for sugary wildflowers to feast on.

The area is also home to a superb range of birds of prey such as kites and eagles soaring overhead looking out for a meal, while myriad timid songbirds provide sonorous entertainment from the safety of tree cover.

GETTING THERE

All four lakes can easily be accessed by overseas visitors. Specific details for getting around locally are given in the introduction to each chapter.

By air

Bergamo's Orio Al Serio airport (www.sacbo.it) is handy for both Lago di Como and Iseo. Milan's Linate and Malpensa airports (www.sea-aeroportimilano.it) also serve Como and Iseo, as well as Lago Maggiore.

For Lago di Garda, Brescia (www. aeroportobrescia.it) or Verona airport (www.aeroportoverona.it) are more convenient.

By train

A couple of international train lines between Switzerland, Austria and Italy come in handy. The Brig to Milano Centrale run via Domodossola calls at Stresa on Lago Maggiore. For Lago di Como there are fast direct trains from Zurich via Chiasso to San Giovanni station at Como, and from there to Milano Centrale. For Lago di Garda a handy stop is Rovereto on the Munich–Innsbruck–Verona railway line as it has good bus links for Riva del Garda (Italian trains, tel. 892021, www.trenitalia.com).

LOCAL TRANSPORT

The extensive network of trains, buses, ferries and cable cars around and across the Italian lakes is easy to use and unfailingly reliable. All the walks in this guidebook start and finish at a point that is accessible by local public transport (and the book was researched by public transport, too). Local drivers know the roads and conditions like the back of their hand, leaving passengers free to sit back and enjoy the views. So visitors never need to think of hiring or taking their own car and so can avoid contributing to air pollution and traffic congestion in these magical places.

Generally speaking bus schedules follow the Italian school year, with extra runs during term time. Slightly reduced summer timetables correspond to the holidays, which fall around mid-June through to mid-September. Full ferry services are timetabled from March/April through to October/November; during winter services are cut back drastically, and some suspended. Exact dates vary from year to year, company to company and region to region, and can be checked on the websites listed under the individual lakes.

Reasonable pricing prevails everywhere: for instance, at the time of writing the ferry from Intra to Laveno on Lago Maggiore costs €3. Over 65s are entitled to reductions (Monday–Friday only). Day tickets are available – ask for *biglietto di libera circolazione* – and fares range from €6.70 to €26.40, depending on the lake and area. A train ticket from Stresa to Belgirate costs €1.50, while the funicular from Como to Brunate is €2.80 one-way or €5.10 return. The cable cars tend to be more expensive: the Malcesine cable car on Lago di Garda costs €16 single, or €18 for the return trip.

Bus tickets should usually be purchased before a journey, either at the bus station or newsstands or tobacconists displaying the appropriate logo for the relevant transport company. Should a railway station be unmanned and have no automatic machine (common at minor stations), ask the conductor on board the train to sell you a ticket.

Specific details for buses, trains, ferries, cable cars and taxis are given at the beginning of each chapter.

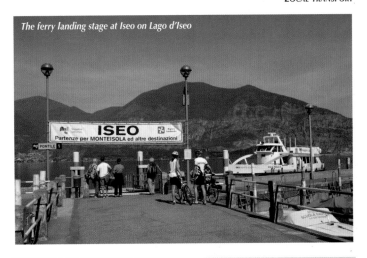

The ferry landing stage at Iseo on Lago d'Iseo

Useful Expressions

These expressions may come in useful when purchasing tickets.

One ticket/two tickets to
    Monteisola, please.
*Un biglietto/due biglietti per
    Monteisola, per favore.*
single   *andata/corsa semplice*
return   *andata ritorno*

How much is that?   *Quanto costa?*
platform   *binario*
timetable   *orario*
Thank you   *Grazie*
You're welcome   *Prego*

The following words may be helpful for understanding timetables.

Cambio a.../coincidenza
Change at.../connection
estivo/invernale   summer/winter
feriale   working days (Monday to
    Saturday)
festivo   holidays (Sundays and
    public holidays)

giornaliero   daily
Lunedì a Venerdì/sabato
    Monday to Friday/Saturday
navetta   shuttle service
sciopero   strike
scolastico   during school term

INFORMATION

The Italian Tourist Board (www.enit.it) has offices all over the world and can help those planning to visit the Italian lakes with general information.

UK 1 Princes Street, London W1B 2AY
Tel. 0207 408 1254
US 630 Fifth Avenue – Suite 1565, New York NY 10111
Tel. 212 2455618
Australia Level 4, 46 Market Street, Sydney, NSW 2000 Tel. 02 92621666

Information on accommodation, transport and what to see can be obtained from local tourist information offices and websites.

A gondola rises to dizzy heights over Laveno on Lago Maggiore (Walk 12)

Lago Maggiore
Cannero Riviera Tel. 0323 788943
www.cannero.it
Cannobio Tel. 0323 71212
www.procannobio.it
Laveno Tel. 0332 668785
www.vareseturismo.it
Luino Tel. 0332 530019
www.vareselandoftourism.it
www.comune.luino.va.it
Stresa Tel. 0323 31308
www.stresaturismo.it
www.visitstresa.com
Verbania: Pallanza Tel. 0323 503249;
Intra Tel. 348 2547482
www.verbania-turismo.it

Lago di Como
Bellagio Tel. 031 951555
www.promobellagio.it

Como Tel. 031 269712
www.lakecomo.it
Domaso Tel. 0344 96322
www.promodomaso.com
Gravedona Tel. 0344 85005
turismo.gravedona@gmail.com
Lecco Tel. 0341 295720
www.turismo.provincia.lecco.it
Menaggio Tel. 0344 32924
www.menaggio.com

Lago d'Iseo
Iseo Tel. 030 980209
www.provincia.brescia.it/turismo
Lovere Tel. 035 962178
www.comune.lovere.bg.it
Peschiera Maraglio, Monteisola
Tel. 030 9825088
www.comune.monteisola.bs.it
www.tuttomonteisola.it
Zone Tel. 030 9880116
www.aprotur.it

Lago di Garda

www.visitgarda.com
Desenzano Tel. 030 3748726
www.provincia.brescia.it/turismo
Gargnano Tel. 0365 791243
www.gargnanosulgarda.it
Limone
Tel. 39 0365 918987/0365 954265
www.visitlimonesulgarda.com
Malcesine Tel. 045 7400044
www.tourism.verona.it
www.malcesinepiu.it
Riva del Garda Tel. 0464 554444
www.gardatrentino.it
San Zeno di Montagna
Tel. 045 6289296
www.comunesanzenodimontagna.it
Torbole Tel. 0464 505177
www.gardatrentino.it
Torri di Benaco Tel. 045 7225120
www.tourism.verona.it

Toscolano-Maderno
Tel. 030 3748741
www.provincia.brescia.it/turismo

WHEN TO GO

The great lakes are renowned for their mild climate. Temperatures range from around 13°C in December to the high 20s in July.

Generally speaking the months of spring through to early summer (April to June) are absolutely perfect and highly recommended for walking in the area as temperatures are usually reasonable, the vegetation is a brilliant green and the flowers blooming. However, September and October are wonderful as well, with marginally fewer visitors and clear crisp conditions once any summer haze

Bellagio and far-off Monte Legnone from the belvedere, Lago di Como (Walk 25)

has dissipated. Midsummer (July and August) can get quite hot – up to 30°C – although an afternoon breeze is nearly always guaranteed. Of course the heat can be tempered by a dip in a lake (or your hotel swimming pool) or better still, a walk to a high altitude.

The high-altitude walking routes are out of bounds throughout the winter months due to snowfalls. However, crisp sunny winter days can make for perfect low-altitude walking with brilliant visibility in the absence of the summer haze.

The lakes can get very busy on the main Italian public holidays: 1 January (New Year), 6 January (Epiphany), Easter Sunday and Monday, 25 April (Liberation Day), 1 May (Labour Day), 2 June (Republic Day), 15 August (Ferragosto), 1 November (All Saints), 8 December (Immaculate Conception), 25–26 December (Christmas and Boxing Day).

Be aware that ferry services are reduced from November through to March, when much accommodation closes, as do villas and gardens.

ACCOMMODATION

A huge range of accommodation in hotels, B&Bs and campsites, and even a couple of hostels and mountain huts, is on offer at all the lakes. Suggestions for options in the middle price range (around €60–100 for a double room with breakfast) are given in the introductions to each chapter; most have websites and accept credit card payments. A deposit will nearly always be required. Book well in advance, especially around the Italian public holidays and the peak months of May and September. For self-catering possibilities contact the Tourist Offices. All the major towns and villages have a grocery store or supermarket, not to mention ATMs.

Remember that many places – but by no means all – close over the winter, usually from October/November to March/April, so check beforehand if planning on a low-season visit.

An overnight stay in a *rifugio* is always a memorable experience. These chalets – set on mountain slopes far from roads and villages, and accessible on foot – are staffed during the summer months and provide reasonably priced meals and dormitory accommodation for walkers and climbers. Contact details are given in the relevant walk descriptions (11, 18, 46 and 47).

If phoning from overseas to book accommodation preface the phone numbers with +39, country code for Italy, and always include the initial 0 of the area code, now incorporated into all Italian phone numbers. If calling from within Italy, dial that 0 as well. The only exceptions are Italian mobile phones which begin with 3, emergency numbers such as 118 for medical matters, or some information services which start 800 (toll-free) or 840 (local call charge).

FOOD AND DRINK

Special treats are in store for the taste buds of adventurous eaters. The four areas featured in this guide are covered by the northern Italian regions of Piemonte, Lombardia, Trentino-Alto Adige and the Veneto, and each proudly nurtures its own gastronomic specialities. Some brief notes are given here to guide visitors, but generally speaking the best rule in a restaurant is to ask for the day's speciality, which will invariably feature seasonal locally sourced products. *Che cosa avete oggi?* means 'What's on today?'

Breakfast in Italy tends to be a simple affair. Most Italians take a coffee as *cappuccino* (with frothy milk) or *espresso* (a strong black concentrated shot), usually accompanied by a croissant, while standing at the local café. These days most middle-range

hotels and B&Bs do a decent buffet breakfast with fruit, cereals, eggs, bread and a choice of beverage.

For picnic lunches, neighbourhood grocery shops or small supermarkets are usually happy to make up a fresh bread roll (*panino*) with your choice of filling. Any of the renowned Italian cured meats, such as *prosciutto crudo*, are perfect. Salami made with goat meat is a variant on the more usual pork. One unparalleled treat found in the mountains of Piemonte is *violino d'agnello*, lamb that has been softened with lard; sliced transparently thin, it melts in the mouth. Cheeses crafted from cow (*mucca*), sheep (*pecora*) or goat (*capra*) milk come in a huge range: soft, smooth, crumbly, tangy (and downright mouldy and stinky at times), as the mouth-watering display at any delicatessen can attest.

On Monte Carza above Lago Maggiore (Walk 8)

In terms of dinner, Lombardia spells risotto heaven and foodies will find plenty to get their forks into. Where available go for the ultimate, *risotto alla milanese*, creamy rice cooked in a delicate meat broth, fragrant with saffron and often twinned with *ossobuco*, tender braised veal shank. Pasta everywhere comes in a bewildering array of shapes and sauces. Unusual choices include Piemontese *panciotti*, pasta parcels stuffed with fish, or *strangolapreti* ('priest stranglers'!), a Trentino dish of small gnocchi dumplings of spinach and potato drizzled with melted butter. On Lago di Garda *tagliolini con cream di limone*, thin ribbons of fresh pasta in a tangy lemon sauce, should be on offer.

In the Brescia district of Lombardia country restaurants do *Spiedo* on the weekend: a selection of meats liberally seasoned with fresh herbs is gently spit roasted and served with *polenta* (cornmeal). Traditionally it also traditionally meant *uccellini*, birds hunted in the hills over the autumn months.

Freshwater fish from all the lakes constantly features on menus. The most common is *coregone* – also known as *lavarello* – which translates as whitefish. Its pale flesh, delicate and soft, is perfectly suited to a quick grilling or frying. Diners on Lago di Como may also be offered *missoltino* or *agone*, a type of small pilchard that has been salted and preserved (the English name is 'twaite shad', a member of the herring family). Look out too for the curiously named fried bleak (*alborelle*), a small silvery lake fish.

An excellent dessert or snack is the Trentino speciality *torta sbrisolona*, a delicious type of crumbly shortbread made with chopped almonds.

Rifugio Menaggio, a welcoming mountain hut offering meals and dormitory accommodation (Walk 18)

Wine lists offer a kaleidoscope of flavours and experiences. Piemonte boasts arguably the best of Italy with memorable reds such as Barbera, Nebbiolo and Dolcetto. In the southern reaches of Lago di Garda, in the Veneto, quaffable reds are copious, starting with Bardolino and Valpolicella that need little introduction, and moving on to more substantial – and stronger in both alcohol and taste – garnet-coloured Recioto and the legendary Amarone: the latter's price tag suggests it be reserved for a very special occasion.

A note on drinking water: Italian domestic tap water (*acqua da rubinetto*) is always safe for drinking (*potabile* means drinkable), and by law is meticulously tested on a frequent basis. You can request it in any restaurant and café instead of bottled mineral water, which needs to be transported at a high cost to the environment. Thankfully there is a growing movement of people aware of and working to avoid such waste. For instance the innovative administrators of the Province of Brescia – from the eastern shore of Lago d'Iseo to the western edge of Lago di Garda – have installed dispensers of free water in towns and villages across their territory; filtered mains water, it comes chilled, fizzy or flat. This is a reinvention of the age-old tradition of the village fountain, still alive and commonplace in the majority of the alpine villages and hamlets visited during these walks.

WHAT TO TAKE

- Sun protection: hat, high-factor cream and sunglasses
- Bottle for drinking water
- Small daypack: shoulder and hand-held bags are unwise, as it's safer to have hands and arms free while walking
- Lightweight trekking boots, or decent pair of trainers or sports shoes, with good grip and thickish soles to protect your feet from loose stones; sandals are quite unsuitable
- Trekking poles for the high mountain routes
- Waterproof gear including lightweight jacket, rucksack cover, and optional overtrousers
- T-shirts and shorts during spring/summer, layered with a light sweater or shirt for cooler conditions
- Autum/winter visitors should pack warm clothes: long trousers, fleece or pullover, hat and gloves
- Basic first-aid kit
- Whistle, headlamp or torch, to be used if calling for help in an emergency
- Maps (see below) and compass

MAPS

Sketch maps are provided for each walk in this guidebook. As much useful detail and key landmarks have been crammed in as possible, dictated by limits of space and graphics. In many cases these are sufficient for the walk, in combination with the walk description. However it is always a good idea to get hold of larger maps of the area for a number of valid reasons: they put places in a wider context, help you identify other points of interest, plot your own routes, and last but not least, are an essential tool for orientation if you lose your way. A decent range of walking maps is available for the lakes, and information concerning specific maps is given in the introduction to each chapter. Some maps are available overseas at outdoor stores and bookshops, several can be downloaded from websites, while others are sold locally at the lakes.

Many grape varieties flourish on sunny slopes around the lakes

DOS AND DON'TS

- Don't set out late in the day, even on a short walk. Always allow extra time for detours and wrong turns.
- Do find time to get in decent shape before setting out on your holiday, as it will maximise enjoyment. The wonderful scenery will be better appreciated when you're not in a state of exhaustion, and healthy walkers react better in an emergency.
- Don't walk on your own. Stick with your companions and don't lose sight of them; remember that the progress of the group should match that of the slowest member.
- Don't be overly ambitious; choose routes suited to your ability (and to that of the group). Read the walk description carefully before setting out.
- Avoid walking in brand new footwear, to reduce the likelihood of blisters; leave those old worn-out shoes at home, as they may be unsafe on slippery terrain. Choose your footwear carefully; comfort is essential.
- Check the weather forecast locally if possible and don't start out even on a short route if storms are forecast: paths can get slippery and mountainsides are prone to rockfalls.
- Carry weatherproof gear at all times, along with food and plenty of drinking water.

- In electrical storms, don't shelter under trees or rock overhangs and keep away from metallic fixtures.
- **Do not** rely on your mobile phone in an emergency as there is often no signal in the mountainous areas.
- Carry any rubbish back to the village where it can be disposed of correctly. Even organic waste such as apple cores and orange peel is best not left lying around as it can upset the diet of animals and birds and irritate other visitors.
- Be considerate if you have to make a toilet stop (and avoid doing so if possible). Keep away from watercourses, burn used paper and bury waste.
- Lastly, don't leave your common sense at home.

EMERGENCIES

For medical matters, EU residents need a European Health Insurance Card (EHIC). Holders are entitled to free or subsidised emergency treatment in Italy, which has an excellent national health service. UK residents can apply online at www.dh.gov.uk. Australia has a similar reciprocal agreement – see www.medicareaustralia.gov.au. Other nationalities should take out suitable equivalent insurance.

Travel insurance for a walking holiday is also strongly recommended, as the costs of rescue and repatriation can be considerable. Members of Alpine clubs are usually covered, but do check before you depart.

The following services may be of help should problems arise.

Walking shoes with a good grip are essential, as seen on the scenic path to Cima delle Pozzette (Walk 44)

Remember that calls made from a public phone require a coin or pre-paid card to be inserted, although no charge is made for short emergency numbers or those starting 800, which are toll-free.

- General emergency Tel. 112
- Polizia (police) Tel. 113
- Health-related emergencies including ambulance (*ambulanza*) and mountain rescue (*soccorso alpino*) Tel. 118
- 'Help!' in Italian is *Aiuto!*, pronounced 'eye-you-tow'. *Pericolo* is 'danger'.

Should help be needed during a walk, use the following internationally recognised rescue signals: **six** signals per minute either visual (waving a handkerchief or flashing a torch) or audible (shouting or whistling), repeated after a pause of one minute. The answer is **three** visual or audible signals per minute, to be repeated after a one-minute pause. Anyone who sees or hears a call for assistance must contact the nearest source of help, a mountain hut or police station for example, as quickly as possible.

These hand signals (below) could be useful for communicating at a distance or with a helicopter.

USING THIS GUIDE

This guidebook contains a selection of the multitude of walking routes on four of the lakes in northern Italy. The aim is to describe the top routes without making the book too cumbersome and encyclopaedic. Visitors wishing to do more – and there is plenty more! – can enquire at the Tourist Offices to join a local guided walk, or invent their own routes with the aid of a good map.

The 48 walks in this guide are suitable for a wide range of holiday-makers. There is something for everyone, from easy leisurely strolls for first-time walkers to strenuous climbs for those with experience up panoramic peaks. Every route has been designed to fit into a single day. Many routes are waymarked with official CAI (Italian Alpine Club) red/white paint stripes together with an identifying number, to be found along the way on prominent stones, trees, walls and rock faces.

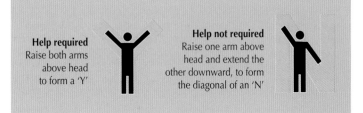

Help required
Raise both arms above head to form a 'Y'

Help not required
Raise one arm above head and extend the other downward, to form the diagonal of an 'N'

There are many different styles of signs to help you on your way!

Each walk description is preceded by an information box containing the following essential data:

- **Start**
- **Finish**
- **Distance** in kilometres and miles.
- **Ascent/Descent**
  Height gain and loss are an indication of effort required and need to be taken into account alongside difficulty and distance when planning the day. Generally speaking, a walker of average fitness will cover 300m (about 1000ft) in ascent in one hour.
- **Difficulty**
  Each walk has been classified by grade, although adverse weather conditions will make any route more arduous.

- *Grade 1* Easy route on clear tracks and paths, suitable for beginners.
- *Grade 2* Paths across hill and mountain terrain, with lots of ups and downs; a reasonable level of fitness is required.
- *Grade 3* Strenuous, entailing some exposed stretches and possibly prolonged ascent. Experience and extra care are recommended.
- **Walking time** This does not include pauses for picnics, views, photos or nature stops, so always add on a good couple of hours when planning your day. Times given during the descriptions are partial (as opposed to cumulative).

The path emerges over Griante above Lago di Como (Walk 15)

- **Access** Information on how to get to the start point and away from the finish point by public and/or private transport.

Within the walk descriptions, 'path' is used to mean a narrow pedestrian-only way, 'track' and 'lane' are unsurfaced but vehicle width, and 'road' is surfaced and open to traffic unless specified otherwise. Compass bearings are in abbreviated form (N, S, NNW and so on) as are right (R) and left (L). Reference landmarks and places encountered en route and shown on the accompanying map are in **bold** type, with altitude in metres above sea level given as 'm', not to be confused with minutes (abbreviated as min). Note that 100m = 328ft.

LAGO MAGGIORE

There are gorgeous views of Cannobio towards the end of Walk 7

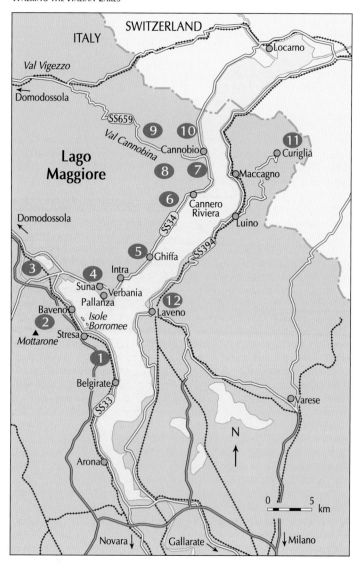

INTRODUCTION

It is the most voluptuous place I have ever seen in the world. Nature enchants you with a thousand unknown fascinations and you feel in a state of rare sensuality and refinement.

Gustave Flaubert, 1845

Picturesque Lago Maggiore has been working its magic on writers and visitors for centuries. Blessed with a mild climate and delightful position close to the Alps, it attracts flocks of admirers to its shores and islands adorned with sumptuous villas and gorgeous ornamental gardens, a legacy of the late Renaissance when the commanding Visconti and Borromeo families were at the height of their powers.

In spite of its denomination *maggiore* ('greatest'), this is not Italy's largest lake, as Garda pips it to the post. Its perimeter runs for 170km and surface area is 212km²; however, its 66km length makes it the country's longest. The lake's western shore belongs to the Italian region of Piemonte, the eastern section is in Lombardia, while the top fifth is Swiss territory.

Beyond the justifiably popular lakefront is a charming string of age-old alpine-style villages dotted over densely wooded mountain slopes and linked by ancient mule tracks and paths. Walks galore! Moreover three of the countless mountains edging the lake are simply sensational belvederes – and two of these have cable cars running up them. The

Mottarone, Monte Carza and Sasso del Ferro are climbed on Walks 2, 8 and 12 respectively.

EXPLORING THE LAKE

The main road SS33 and the Milan–Domodossola railway line travel north from **Arona** on the southeastern shore to the pretty village of **Belgirate**, conclusion of Walk 1. A quiet stretch of wooded shoreline continues to **Stresa** (Tourist Office Tel. 0323 31308 www.stresaturismo.it, www.visitstresa.com). 'I'm up here at Stresa a little resort on Lake Maggiore, one of the most beautiful of the Italian Lakes,' wrote Ernest Hemingway in 1929.

Without a doubt this is the best-visited town on Lago Maggiore – and with excellent reason. Apart from its beautiful waterfront lined with magnificent *belle époque* villas surrounded by immaculate parkland, it boasts easy access to the trio of world-famous Isole Borromee: Isola Bella, Isola dei Pescatori and Isola Madre. These tiny gem-like islands are jam-packed with exquisite gardens and villas. Charles Dickens wrote (1844), 'For however fanciful and fantastic

Sasso del Ferro from the Stresa waterfront (Walk 1)

the Isola Bella may be, and is, it still is beautiful.'

As well as plenty of ferries, frequent trains on the main Milan–Domodossola line stop at Stresa, while SAF buses provide a link with Verbania and a shuttle service for Milan's Malpensa airport. The many accommodation options include Albergo Sempione, aka Hotel Simplon (Tel. 0323 30463, www.albergosempione.it) and Hotel Elena (Tel. 0323 3339, www.hotelelena.com).

From the Lido di Stresa, also referred to as Carciano, a two-stage cable car swings inland up the gently sloping Mottarone, an alpine belvedere *par excellence* with a breathtaking panorama. Walk 2 explores the mountain, while Walk 1 takes a stroll through the woods south of Stresa.

The next location of interest is **Baveno**, a quiet lakeside location served by SAF buses and ferries across to the islands and Verbania. Walk 2 concludes here (Hotel Beau Rivage Tel. 0323 924534, www.beaurivage-baveno.com).

After Baveno the lake shore swings into the delta of the River Toce at Fondotoce, a nature reserve. Campsites abound such as Campeggio Lido Toce (Tel. 0323 496220, www.campinglidotoce.eu). This rectangular body of water is often referred to as the Borromean Gulf, after the islands. Monteorfano, a curious lump of granite explored in Walk 3, dominates the landscape here. The railway line then curves northwest and calls in at Pallanza-Verbania station where Walk 3 begins, before proceeding on for Domodossola. A VCO bus transports passengers from the station to Pallanza proper and other parts of Verbania.

Verbania is the name for the whole of the promontory but there are several ports of call, all served by ferry and SAF and VCO buses. The first is **Suna**, a nice place to stay a short detour off the busy main road (Hotel Pesce D'Oro Tel. 0323 504445, www.hotelpescedoro.it). Walk 4 starts here. A short drive above Suna stands the pretty village of **Cavandone**, reached on Walk 4 as well as by VCO bus. Here you can stay at B&B Casa Musto (Tel. 0323 557703).

Next and closest to the point is **Pallanza** with a Tourist Office (Tel 0323 503249, www.verbania-turismo.it), pedestrian district, beach and plenty of hotels. There's also a

Youth Hostel (Tel. 0323 501648 www.ostelloverbania.com). Pallanza is well served by ferries which shuttle across to the Borromean islands. Just around the point to the north is renowned Villa Taranto with its simply magnificent gardens (www.villataranto.it).

Intra acts as the port of call for the mid-lake car and passenger ferry across to Laveno and ferries from all over the lake. It is also an important terminal for SAF services from Stresa and beyond, as well as the VCO bus runs from Domodossola and north to the Swiss border and Brissago. Intra has an interesting old town and makes an excellent base for visiting this central part of the lake, with plenty of good restaurants and hotels such as Intra Hotel (Tel. 0323 581393) or Miralago (Tel. 0323 404080), both at www.verbaniahotel.it. A kiosk (Tel.

Isola Bella

A ferry arrives at Cannero Riviera (Walk 7)

348 2547482) near the ferry wharves acts as the tourist information point.

The SS34 narrows rather as it passes through **Ghiffa**, a modest line-up of shops and houses on the lakefront, which acts as the key gateway for the Sacro Monte sanctuary route (Walk 5).

On a rounded promontory of fluvial deposit jutting out onto the lake, **Cannero Riviera** is set off the main road and boasts a decent albeit shingle beach (campsite Camping al Lido Tel. 0323 787148, www.campinglidocannero.com). The lakefront promenade is a line-up of inviting restaurants and elegant upmarket hotels. Handy for the bus stop is peaceful family-run B&B Casa al Mulino (Tel. 0323 787197, www.casaalmulino.it), while grocery shops and the friendly Tourist Office (Tel. 0323 788943, www.cannero.

it) are a short way downhill. Walks 6 and 7 start at Cannero Riviera. Quiet B&B Casale is located at Cassino, a short distance above the town and visited during Walk 6 (Tel. 0323 739708, www.bedandbreakfastlagomaggiore. it). The local taxi can be contacted on Tel. 348 9046323.

Utterly charming **Cannobio** has a long pedestrian lakefront, especially animated of a Sunday for the weekly market that draws crowds from far and wide. Set off the road, the village has a historic heart with paved alleys and elegant palazzi as well as a well-stocked Tourist Office (Tel. 0323 71212, www. procannobio.it). Accommodation possibilities include centrally located B&B 21 (Tel. 0323 71685, www.b-b21. it) and Albergo del Fiume (Tel. 0323 739121, www.hoteldelfiume.it). Walks 8 and 10 begin here.

Branching due west from Cannobio is the beautiful wild **Val Cannobina** that snakes its tortuous way up to join Val Vigezzo. It is explored in Walk 9; there is B&B accommodation at Orasso (Pensione Belvedere Tel. 0323 77136), and Cavaglio (home stay Tel. 340 5283765).

Infrequent VCO buses reach the villages, but at rather inconvenient times for walkers, so the Cannobio taxi service (Tel. 0323 71410, Mob. 348 7821699) may come in handy.

Immediately north of Cannobio and Brissago the top end of the lake enters Swiss territory, curving northeast to Locarno, and is not explored in this guidebook. On the other side of the water, not far south of the international border, the SS394 runs through the township of **Luino**. This town has good ferry links across to the western shore and Cannobio and Cannero, as well as rail links with Switzerland, and south via Gallarate to Milan. While it somehow lacks the charm of the Piemonte villages, its great draw is the Wednesday market, when the whole town is invaded by long lines of stalls and huge numbers of shoppers who flock here for bargains. Luino is handy for Walk 11 as the Baldioli bus to Curiglia starts out from here. Hotels include Hotel Del Pesce (Tel. 0332 532379, www.hoteldelpesce.it) and old-style Ancora (Tel 0332 530451, www.hotelancoraluino.com), and there's a helpful Tourist Office (Tel. 0332 530019, www.vareselandof-tourism.itwww.comune.luino.va.it).

The next useful place is **Laveno**, 16km south, linked to Intra by the mid-lake passenger and vehicle ferry. A modest spot with a good Tourist Office (Tel. 0332 668785, www.vareseturismo.it), it is the gateway to the Sasso del Ferro mountain (Walk 12) and its curious *bidonvia* open-sided cable car that runs daily March–November. This town also hosts a bustling weekly market (Tuesdays), a legacy from the days when Laveno was the centre of the cereal trade. Accommodation is available at Hotel Meublé Moderno (Tel. 0332 668373, www.meublemoderno.it). Trains on the Ferrovie Nord line from Milano Cadorna terminate here.

The old part of Cannobio (Walk 7)

MAPS

The Kompass map 1:50,000 n.90 Lago Maggiore is fine for general orientation and planning, and covers all the routes except for Walk 3. However, it is lacking in local detail and is often inaccurate, so use a local map where possible.

A decent 1:30,000 map of the paths around Stresa (useful for Walks 1 and 2) can be downloaded from www.stresaturismo.it. Tourist Offices including Luino and Laveno in the Province of Varese can provide the free map 'Via Verde Varesina' Istituto Geografico De Agostini 1:35,000, good for Walks 11 and 12.

For Walks 6, 7, 8, 9, 10 there's the Cartine Zanetti 1:30,000 sheet n.58 'Cannobio, Cannero Riviera' on sale locally.

TRANSPORT

- Baldioli buses
  Tel. 0332 530271
  www.baldioli.it
- Ferrovie Nord
  Tel. 800 500005
  www.ferrovienord.it
- Ferry timetables
  Tel. 800 551801
  www.navlaghi.it
- Italian State Trains
  Tel. 892021
  www.trenitalia.com
- Laveno cable car
  Tel. 0332 668012
  www.funiviedellagomaggiore.it
- Mottarone cable car
  Tel. 0323 30295
  www.stresa-mottarone.it
- SAF buses
  Tel. 0323 552172
  www.safduemila.com
- VCO buses
  Tel. 0323 518711
  www.vcotrasporti.it

WALK 1

Stresa to Belgirate

Start	Stresa Tourist Office, Piazza Marconi
Finish	Belgirate railway station
Distance	9km (5.6 miles)
Ascent/Descent	300m/270m
Difficulty	Grade 1–2
Walking time	2hr 30min
Access	Stresa can be reached by train and is well served by ferries which moor at Piazza Marconi alongside the Tourist Office. From Belgirate, trains back to Stresa are approximately hourly, more frequent than ferries.

A string of old pathways, possibly of ancient Roman origin, link the lovely town of Stresa with quiet Belgirate, a little-visited lakeside village to the south. Waymarked as L2, most of the way it passes through divine chestnut woods, with clearings offering inspirational lake views. The chestnut fruit was once fundamental to this area's economy and is referred to as *arbul* – in the local dialect: 'the tree' – *par excellence*. Harvesting the nuts and maintaining man-made terraces is a thing of the past now, but plenty of reminders can still be seen along the way. This is an easy and very enjoyable half-day walk, with a return to Stresa either by ferry or train.

Before setting out get a ferry or train timetable from the Tourist Office and arm yourself with drinking water and a snack as there is nothing in the way of cafés or restaurants until Belgirate.

From lakefront Piazza Marconi and the **Tourist Office** (200m) at **Stresa**, go L (SSE) away from the town along the water's edge as far as the café Pasticceria Gigi. Here turn R on Via Rosmini (red/white waymarks) in gentle ascent past houses and a church, then go L on Via Castello. This becomes a grassy path alongside a stone wall and soon joins a paved old way in ascent to a cluster of houses.

At an intersection with a shrine, fork L on Via Vecchia per Passera, a shady cobbled lane leading SSE into woodland along the boundary of the Villa Pallavicini gardens. It narrows to a good path accompanied by a stream, and climbs steadily, maintaining the same direction. Further along, a house or two is passed and a minor road crossed, then it's up to a wonderful belvedere at the **Oratorio di Passera** (320m), a modest church erected in the 1700s by a local wine merchant to give thanks for deliverance after being shipwrecked on the lake. A quiet surfaced road then a lane lead ahead and there are beautiful views to the opposite shore and the Sasso del Ferro mountain above Laveno.

Ignore the fork L for 'Sentiero dei Castagni' and continue along to a short stretch of road up to the picturesque church and cemetery of **Sant'Albino** (370m, 1hr 15min). Don't take the fork for Magognino but keep straight ahead for a beautiful section on a wide path through ancient chestnut trees, old terracing and huge fallen boulders. At a junction with a shrine, keep L as per the red/white signs and onto a lane through to a vineyard and the pretty hamlet of **Falchetti** in a scenic spot. There's more gentle uphill before a worthwhile 5min detour to a clearing and the 12th-century chapel of **San Paolo**.

The lakefront at Stresa

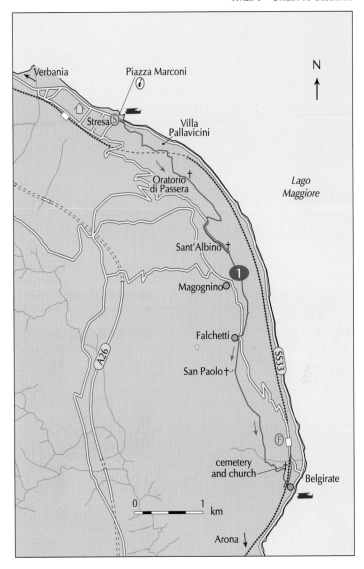

On the way to Belgirate

Back on the main path, in a little while you begin a gradual descent. After crossing the stream Rio San Paolo the path moves out to fields and views towards the lower lake, including the vast line-up of moraine ridges extending east around Varese. A minor road with a tongue-twisting name (Via Pore Musolischvili) leads you to a bridge crossing – then you fork sharp L to where the path resumes as a lovely stepped way. Down at a road turn R and almost straightaway L at a shrine. A flight of steps concludes at the cemetery and Romanesque frescoed church, which boasts an elegant bell tower.

Keep down the paved road, following it as it veers L under the railway line. Then either continue down to the lakeside and ferry wharf, or go L along the road a further 10min to the **railway station** of **Belgirate** (230m, 1hr 15min).

WALK 2

Start	Stresa cable car, Lido di Stresa
Finish	Baveno ferry wharf
Distance	15km (9.3 miles)
Descent	1300m
Difficulty	Grade 2+
Walking time	3hr 45min (+ 20min for lift rides)
Access	Stresa is well served by trains and ferries which moor at the Carciano wharf (Lido di Stresa); otherwise from the centre of Stresa it's a beautiful 15min walk along the lakeside to the *funivia*/cable car. Baveno has frequent ferries back to Stresa.

The route begins with the popular mechanised ascent, a memorable experience for the spectacular vistas over lake and Alps. It's advisable to purchase the combined cable-car/chair lift (*funivia/seggiovia*) ticket all the way to the top. The walk is a very long descent but there's plenty of variety in terms of landscape and terrain with woodland and pasture. The day concludes at utterly charming Baveno. From here you catch a ferry back to Stresa via those fairy-tale islands Isola dei Pescatori and Isola Bella that you've been admiring all day. Meals and refreshments are available at the top of the Mottarone as well as at the Alpino cable-car station halfway down, while an Agriturismo eatery is located at Alpe Cristina, in an especially panoramic spot (check opening times with the Tourist Office in advance).

If the complete walk looks too long for comfort, take a variant: either conclude at Alpino and the botanical garden (www.giardinoalpinia.it), well worth a visit, or ride the cable car from Stresa to Alpino and start there by following the detour to pick up the main route for Baveno.

From **Lido di Stresa** (200m) the cable car makes a spectacular lakeside departure on its two-stage trip to the **Mottarone station** (1378m). A chair lift climbs the final leg to the actual 1491m top of **Mottarone** where an amazing panorama awaits.

THE MOTTARONE

The mountain called the Mottarone is invisible from the famous resort town of Stresa, largely because your attention is naturally drawn to the lake busy with motor boats ferrying visitors around the pretty islands. However, rising above is a sprawling mountain that peaks some distance inland. Isolated between Lago Maggiore and Lago d'Orta, it is one of those apparently nondescript yet extraordinary lookouts that takes your breath away, especially if you're lucky enough to be there when the cool north wind is blowing, sweeping all trace of cloud from the alpine line-up, allowing multi-peaked Monte Rosa to stand out in all its glaciated glory. Also a modest winter ski resort, the Mottarone can be accessed almost year-round by a two-stage cable car, successor of a 1911–1960s cogwheel railway with electric traction, the original route of which is followed during the walk.

On the summit of Mottarone

In optimum conditions a huge **360° arc of the Alps** can be admired, starring Monte Rosa to the west, and pyramidal Monviso in the distance to the southwest. Closer at hand, at your feet, is Lago d'Orta, with Varese to the east.

From the summit cross take the stony path N down grassy slopes bright with gentians, heather and blueberries. Rowan trees line the way as you reach a lane and turn R for the cable-car station and hotel/restaurant Eden (1378m, 15min).

A large yellow sign for path L1 'Sentiero Stresa-Mottarone' points you down a lane, keeping L of the cable-car station with gorgeous views N to the light grey crests of the Val Grande beyond Verbania. The path passes under the cables for the first of several times, and

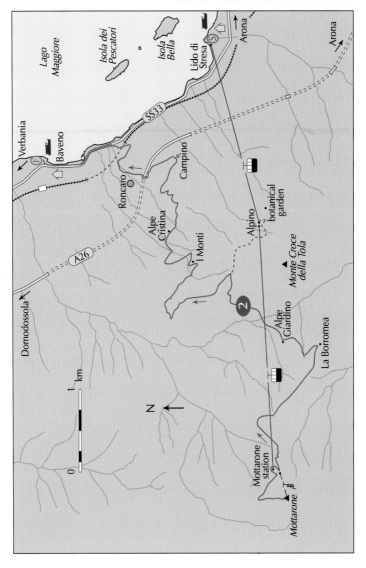

43

heads down into conifer and mixed woodland, home to hundreds of songbirds. It's stony underfoot – watch those ankles. You're guided by occasional red/white and L1 waymarks, and all the junctions are clearly marked.

A long straight stretch SE with a constant gradient is clearly recognisable as the old cogwheel train line, rails long removed. At times the way is sunken with embankments, at others it is built up. A clearing close to the surfaced road corresponds to the former station of **La Borromea** (981m, 45min). Here L1 veers L (NW) on a more leisurely earth-based track through beech woodland. Abandoned houses stand at **Alpe Giardino** (960m) on the edge of a tall dark conifer wood.

Down through clearings you reach a lane and turn R (still NE) beneath the cable car again and past yellow poles for the underground *metanodotto* (gas pipeline). At a T-junction fork L and follow the lane as it circles Monte Croce della Tola, and joins a wider level lane at a rusty metal bar (40min).

If you are interested in going to Alpino, then fork R here as follows.

Detour to Alpino

The lane leads SE through wood, gradually dropping to horse-riding farms, a modest café-restaurant, the renowned Alpine Botanical Garden and the cable-car station of **Alpino** (800m) with great lake views. Allow 10min in descent or 30min in the opposite direction.

At the rusty metal bar go L, as per red/white waymarking for M5. A leisurely level stretch runs through silver birch, which soon thin out for superb views over Lago Maggiore and to the Verbania peninsula. Where you encounter the *metanodotto* (gas pipeline) the lane veers R and down to a junction overlooking the Toce delta and the beautiful sharp granite peaks of the Val Grande. Turn R (SE) towards pasture and groups of old rural buildings (**I Monti**), and onto a minor surfaced road. Not far along you need to fork L (signed for Baveno) through woods for 10min. At the next lane branch R through to the stunning position

of the Agriturismo L'Ordin restaurant at **Alpe Cristina** (630m), an amazing place with spectacular views over the renowned Borromean islands, Verbania and the northern lake.

Lago d'Orta from the top of Mottarone

An old path lined with stone walling plunges through beautiful beech woods dotted with old huts. Look carefully for red/white waymarks at the junctions, and you'll soon reach the first buildings of the pretty, peaceful village of **Campino** (390m, 1hr 10min).

At a drinking tap, branch L down steps through old houses and take Via A Stoppani to the church. Go L across the road to a sign for Baveno, and take the lane Via Madonna della Neve lined with shrines. It reverts to a lane in woodland and curves close to a tunnel in the motorway, quickly left behind. Through a residential area now, the way continues diagonally downhill, ducking below a new house and into woods once more where old cobblestones reappear. This ends at a road where you turn R to quiet **Roncaro** (260m). Near the church fork L down Via Roncaro, a paved lane leading to the main lakeside road SS33. Go L, and it's not far to pick up the beautiful lakeside promenade into charming **Baveno** (200m, 1hr).

WALK 3

Monte Orfano and Lago di Mergozzo

Start/Finish	Pallanza railway station
Distance	13km (8 miles)
Ascent/Descent	600m/600m
Difficulty	Grade 2–3
Walking time	4hr
Access	The railway station for Pallanza on the Milan–Stresa–Domodossola line can also be reached by regular VCO buses linking it with Pallanza and the rest of Verbania. Mergozzo is an alternative entry point – buses on the VCO Domodossola–Verbania run stop at the lakefront piazza. By car, park either near the railway station or at Montorfano.

This walk is a fascinating circuit well away from any industrial activity, but one that touches on the historical military constructions of the Linea Cadorna – see Introduction – and follows many perfectly graded tracks of clear military origin from that time. The summit of Monte Orfano is a belvedere *par excellence*, not to mention a superb spot for watching birds of prey. The woods, on the other hand, are home to colourful jays and noisy nutcrackers.

It's a nice variation to make the detour to Mergozzo and its eponymous lake – or use the tracks as alternative access/exit. In any case take plenty of drinking water and picnic supplies. You could always plan on dropping in to Mergozzo for refreshments, although you may not get there until mid afternoon.

From the **Pallanza railway station** (199m) walk down the road past a pink house to a car park close to the SS34 and a quarry. At the sign for Montorfano fork R on the quiet road, past store yards, to climb gently L (NW). After a couple of bends you pass the A56 path (the return route from Mergozzo). Keep on past the cemetery and up to **Montorfano** (334m, 30min), which boasts an exceptionally handsome Romanesque church.

MONTE ORFANO, MONTORFANO AND MONT'ORFANO

Monte Orfano – as the name suggests – is an 'orphaned mount', a mass of granite that separates tiny Lago Mergozzo from the River Toce which flows down the Ossola valley and into the Borromean Gulf and Lago Maggiore close to the Verbania promontory. The district has been renowned since medieval times for its prized marble and white and green granite, in great demand and fashioned into columns for churches in Rome such as San Paolo fuori le Mura. Even as late as 1830 Monte Orfano boasted 39 quarries, a handful of which are still operating today.

Be aware that the village on the eastern flank of the mountain is called Montorfano (also spelt Mont'Orfano), which can be a little confusing.

Without entering the village, take the signed path A56 which branches R; remnant patches of asphalt suggest it was once a road. As it curves W through the wood, gaps in the foliage offer views over Pallanza to Monterosso, then soon to Lago di Mergozzo.

Heading NW, the path becomes an atmospheric old military track with a perfect gradient through

Lago di Mergozzo and the River Toce from the ascent

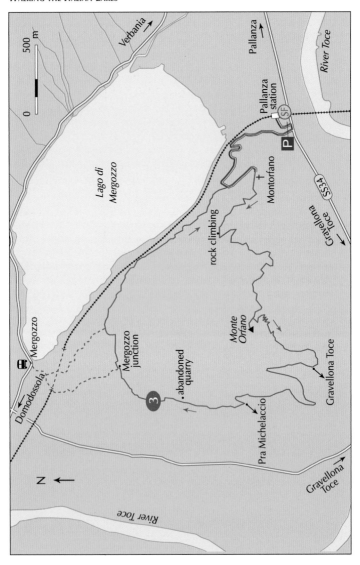

chestnut woods and with plentiful red/white way-marks. After curving L past a rock-climbing area, it reaches a level stretch with fallen rocks. The way narrows here and you need to clamber over several slabs. Further up the path flanks a curious long ramp that concludes at excellent lookouts over the River Toce to the Mottarone W. After a series of grassy terraces with silver birch trees then oak, pass a repeater aerial to come across surprisingly vast military structures connected with the Linea Cadorna, and including underground premises and fortifications.

At a signposted junction go R for the actual flat *cima* (summit) of **Monte Orfano** (794m, 1hr 15min), marked by a stone pillar on an outcrop.

> Not a bad spot for a picnic, this **belvedere** dominates the Ossola valley running northwest and backed by glaciated alpine peaks, the fork south-southwest to Lago d'Orta, the stark crests of the Val Grande standing out to the north, and Lago Maggiore, with Stresa and the islands. No wonder it was considered strategic for the military!

Return to the signposted junction and fork R on the A58 (sign for Mergozzo) for the start of a remarkable military track – innumerable zigzags SW on a stone-edged path in almost imperceptible descent through chestnut woodland. Very slow progress in terms of descent, but at least it is kind on the knees! Ruined stone buildings are dotted along the way, and a broad saddle thick with gorse and ferns passed. Soon the path veers sharp R down to a signed fork where you ignore the turn-off left for Gravellona Toce, and keep straight ahead. The road-width track heads N at first before a long swing SW and past another turn-off (to Pra Michelaccio). A little farther on, soon after a small abandoned quarry, take care not to miss the red/white-marked fork R off the lane for a clear path through old chestnut allotments. It's not far down to a couple of gnarled chestnut trees at the key **Mergozzo junction** (216m, 1hr 30min).

Unless you opt for the detour, go R (E) here, and you're soon joined by the return path from Mergozzo.

Detour to Mergozzo (15min)
From the junction, go L to a shrine marked for 'Mergozzo Lago'. Follow red/white waymarks carefully through lanes and alleys, over the railway line, past a tiny church and finally R downhill (past Via Montorfano/Sentiero Azzurro, the alternative access route – see below) to lakeside Piazza Cavour with cafés and the bus stop at **Mergozzo** (196m).

To rejoin the main route, from the bus stop in Piazza Cavour on the lake's edge, go R (SW) up Via G Borzoni, then immediately L on Via Nostrani. Continue up to where a stepped cobbled way, Via Montorfano aka Sentiero Azzurro/A56, branches L. Not far along at a shrine ignore the fork for Oriola and keep on past houses into wood. An old path lined with stone walls leads to the main route.

The view from Montorfano embraces the Gridoni and the Alps

Leading SE is a beautiful paved lane with benches for admiring Lago di Mergozzo. A delightful stroll, above the railway line as well, it climbs gently to meet the road to Montorfano (30min). Now fork L down the tarmac to return to the **Pallanza railway station** (199m, 15min).

WALK 4

Cavandone on Monterosso

Start/Finish	Suna bus stop at the ferry wharf
Distance	8.5km (5.3 miles)
Ascent/Descent	265m/265m
Difficulty	Grade 1–2
Walking time	2hr 30min
Access	Suna gets frequent SAF buses on the Stresa–Verbania run as well as VCO buses linking Domodossola with Verbania. Few ferries call in. Cavandone is served by VCO bus from Pallanza.

This pleasant loop walk crosses the southern flanks of Monterosso, the mountainous outcrop which dominates the promontory of Verbania halfway up Lago Maggiore. Old mule tracks with intricate paving and remarkably intact drystone walls are followed. The highest point, Cavandone, has superb views over Lago Maggiore and the surrounding mountains. The original layout of this pretty village is still evident: narrow streets and alleys lined with splendid palazzi constructed during the 1700s. It boasts a permanent (albeit small) population (including dozens of cats), and merits an exploratory wander.

Suna has plenty of restaurants, cafés and grocery shops, but there is nothing to eat at Cavandone so stock up on picnic supplies before setting out.

From the bus stop at **Suna** (200m) walk along the lakeside drive to the Hotel Pesce D'Oro then turn R up Via Solferino. This pedestrian alley leads past shops to Via dei Partigiani where you go L through the old part of the village with arched courtyards and shuttered houses. You soon take a *sottopassaggio* (underpass) to duck beneath the main road in the company of the Rio Molinaccio stream. Turn L along Via XX Settembre then branch L again on Via del Buon Rimedio, a narrow surfaced way NW. Lined by high stone walls and rock faces, it climbs

Cavandone is a quiet place

peacefully past well-kept homes shaded by huge trees and lush gardens overflowing with jasmine and roses. There is occasional red/white waymarking.

At a **signboard** a paved path takes over in the same direction, a gentle ascent through beautiful parkland and woods thick with honeysuckle. A wooden bridge precedes **La Torraccia**, a marvellous medieval tower that overlooks the Borromean Gulf; unfortunately it is private property but can be admired from behind a fence. The path becomes marginally steeper and features a couple of erratic boulders deposited there long ago by glaciers. It's not far to the disused 18th-century **Buon Rimedio church** in a clearing with great views across to the Mottarone, not to mention Stresa and the Borromean islands.

Such trees were evidently originally planted at burial places by ancient peoples such as the Celts, to protect the dead.

From the building it's only a matter of metres along the tarmac road then the old way resumes, passing orchards and a plant nursery, guided by white arrows. A string of old shrines dot the way up to the 12th-century Chiesa di Cavandone, with a stupendous **yew tree** believed to be 600 years old! ◄

Cross the road and take the flight of steps into the old village. At a frescoed shrine fork R on the paved alley

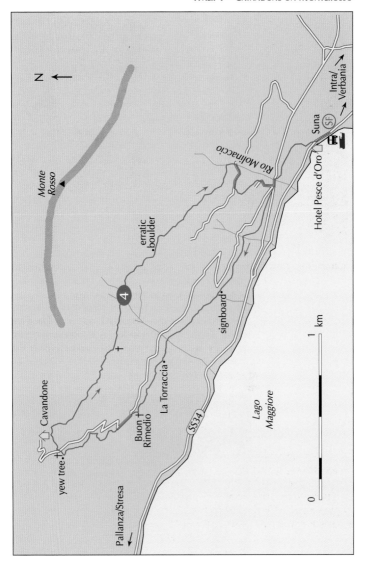

Via del Torchio to an oil press (*torchio*), then continue up to a well in a tiny pretty square in **Cavandone** (440m, 1hr 15min). Do take time out for an exploratory wander through this charming village.

As signed, fork R (E) on Via Sardegna past an especially elegant palazzo from the early 1700s. You soon leave Cavandone behind and head along a lane into woodland alternating with fields and stone walls. After a shrine smothered in honeysuckle comes a brief uphill stretch through parkland then the way narrows to a path, blue paint splashes showing the way. An unusual concentration of glossy dark green cherry laurel bushes accompanies the descent. Just after a minor stream crossing, on your L is a smallish **erratic boulder** whose surface is pitted with tiny holes fashioned by human hands in a long-gone era; no plausible explanation has been found for them.

Soon a lane near houses takes over from the path. Continue in the same direction past a stone cross on a rock outcrop, to where the path resumes at a gate. Steadily downhill it touches on a string of ruined stone huts and plunges into the valley of Rio Molinaccio. At a minor surfaced road turn R to where the path resumes L. This section may be a bit overgrown. Amid houses it joins a steep surfaced road in descent and quickly reaches Via XX Settembre and the underpass. Return to the lakefront and **Suna** (200m, 1hr 15min).

The lakefront at Suna

WALK 5
Ghiffa Sanctuary Loop

Start/Finish	Ghiffa bus stop at the ferry wharf
Distance	10.5km (6.5 miles)
Ascent/Descent	565m/565m
Difficulty	Grade 1–2
Walking time	3hr
Access	Ghiffa is on the VCO bus line between Verbania and Cannobio, and occasional ferries call here. Cars can be driven as far as the Sacro Monte sanctuary.

The walk described here is an easy loop that takes in the peaceful Sacro Monte before wandering through the woods and embarking on a panoramic traverse back to the Sacro Monte sanctuary. Easy lanes are followed the whole way (Grade 1), with the exception of the climb from the Sacro Monte up to the crest, only marginally more difficult (Grade 2). There are café-restaurants at the Ghiffa lakeside, Ronco and the Sacro Monte.

▶ From the bus stop close to the ferry wharf at Ghiffa (198m) walk NNW (Cannero direction) along the promenade. Very shortly you need to cross the road L to take the stepped alley Via Volta alongside the PT (post office). There are faded signs for 'percorso pedonale' (pedestrian route). The path winds uphill passing houses and walled gardens, continuing L on Via Motti to a road. Here fork R past old-style Hotel Paradiso and up to the panoramic village of **Ronco** (280m) and a café-restaurant.

Straight over the road take the flight of steps, keeping L past the cream façade of Chiesa della Visitazione. Another L will see you on the alley Via Torino (sign 'Al Santuario'). Soon turn R up Via Careghetta past gardens, keep R at a Y-junction and onto a shady lane. Climbing steadily this enters pine and chestnut woodland. Ignore the fork R, and keep straight on for the **Sacro Monte sanctuary** aka **SS Trinità** (380m, 30min).

The area is also a special nature reserve, taking in the eastern flanks of Monte Cargiago – a good walking map can be downloaded from **www.sacromonteghiffa.it**.

THE SACRO MONTE OF GHIFFA

In the 15–16th centuries, fanned by a burning desire for a 'New Jerusalem', a curious religious fashion – to recreate scenarios from the Bible – swept across the alpine foothills of Piemonte and Lombardia. Life-size statues from the time of Christ, Mary and the saints populate scale reproductions of locations from the Holy Land. Rather kitsch to modern eyes, the 'Sacro Monte' (holy mountain) installations continue to be places of meditation and pilgrimage as well as venues for village fairs. The Sacro Monte of Ghiffa was constructed in full Baroque splendour during the 1700s, and is included in the group of nine awarded World Heritage status by UNESCO. Modest shrines also dot the mountainside and woods, and act as handy landmarks for walkers.

Four chapels, a colonnaded walkway adorned with plaster reliefs that acts as the Via Crucis, and terracotta statues can be admired at the **sanctuary**, along with lake views. Close by are car parks, café-restaurant and a toilet block.

From the uppermost car park and a map board take path n.18 which climbs N at first. Faded red/white waymarks on rocks and trees lead you up to a path junction to fork L on n.18. Not far along n.18 branches R (W) as a path that climbs steadily. Ignore the link for Porale, and keep upwards, more and more steeply through beautiful chestnut woodland to the shrine, **Cappella della Sabbia Rossa** (640m). It dates all the way back to 1690 and still boasts a fresco, albeit faded and fragmented. Not far uphill from here you gain the wooded ridge from Monte Cargiago and a **path junction** (715m, 45min). Don't branch R for Pollino but go straight ahead on n.18b which leads in gentle descent N to a clearing and the huts of **Usceno** (695m) for a wider track through to a major lane, n.1 in Valle di Pollino.

Branch L (SW), accompanied by the Rio Ballona stream and plenty of songbirds via the **Cappella di Monte** shrine (600m). Keep on down to a road and branch L through the quiet village **Caronio** (494m) that enjoys views to the Mottarone behind Stresa as well as Lago

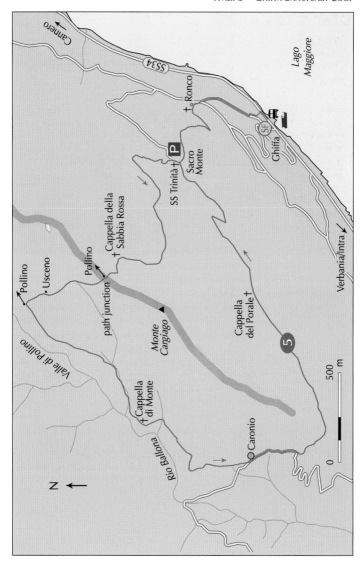

Ghiffa sanctuary overlooks the lake

Maggiore. At a sharp curve R in the road, at a traffic mirror, fork L, signed for the Santuario della Trinità. Buildings are quickly left behind on this absolutely beautiful stretch heading NE, a level stroll amidst scented broom and myriad Mediterranean flowers and bushes, with fantastic views across the glittering lake. It's a gentle descent and you eventually enter cool conifer forest with **Cappella della Porale** (470m). Further along the lane are picnic tables, then the **SS Trinità** (380m, 1hr 15min) once again.

As per the ascent, fork R down the steps and back to **Ronco** and then the lakeside at **Ghiffa** (198m), with ferry wharf and bus stop.

WALK 6
Villages above Cannero

Start/Finish	Cannero Riviera bus stop
Distance	16.5km (10.3 miles)
Ascent/Descent	800m/800m
Difficulty	Grade 2 (short stretch Grade 3)
Walking time	4hr
Access	Cannero Riviera is served by frequent VCO buses; the bus stop is on the main road 5min from the lakefront, where ferries call in. Trarego has a VCO bus service, handy for a variant exit.

This very rewarding circuit walk begins as a lakeside promenade around the fluvial fan that hosts Cannero Riviera, then climbs gently through a series of villages, each with characteristic stone-roofed buildings, and even the occasional stately villa. After the belvedere of Oggiogno comes a tricky but short stretch where the path narrows and plunges to avoid a landslide. Once Rio Cannero has been crossed the old gentle way resumes to Trarego. Located on the south-facing flanks of the Monte Carza–Pian Bello line-up, it is one of the rare inhabited mountain villages that still boasts a grocery store and bus service.

There are modest café-restaurants at both Oggiogno and Trarego, otherwise buy a *panino* beforehand at Cannero. All the villages have drinking fountains.

From the bus stop at **Cannero Riviera** (197m) turn downhill on Via Dante Alighieri. At the lakeside promenade (the ferry wharf is a short distance to the left) go R past a marina and campsite then along the shingle beach. Keep L past a café and onto a path following the water's edge. At the end fork R up to the road near Hotel Rondinella. Taking great care with the traffic, follow the road L for a matter of metres to steps R (sign for Cassino). You bear L below a house to the start of an old paved mule track SW dotted with shrines. Accompanied by gorgeous lake views it reaches peaceful **Cassino** (45min).

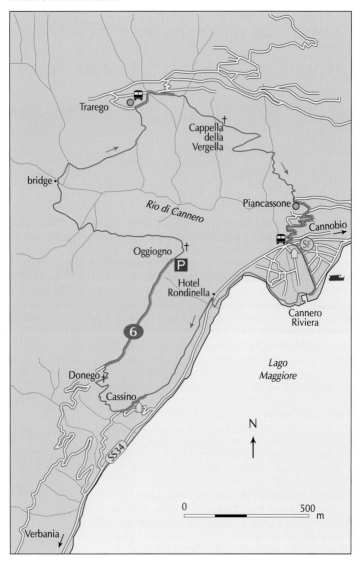

An alley leads past B&B Casale to the church, where you branch R on a cobbled path. Tight zigzags NW enter woodland then cross a surfaced road, to pass through an area of landslip where path and road have been reconstructed. With occasional red/yellow waymarks, you soon reach **Donego** (420m, 20min), a tranquil tiny hamlet, its *osteria* (bar) long closed. Fork R to the belvedere and church with a shady portico and stone benches. Not far along is a drinking tap where you need to fork L under an ancient arch at house n.26 for steep well-worn steps cut into the rock. Further up fork R along the quiet road and stick with it to **Oggiogno** (515m, 30min), a favourite summer haunt of swifts. ▶

Set on a dramatic outcrop in the shadow of triangular Cima di Morissolo to the west and Monte Carza to the northeast, the village is a superb lookout.

Walk past the car park and through to Piazza dei Terrieri alongside the church, where elegant villas and gardens flank a jumble of old stone-roofed dwellings. Turn L down the alley with the gushing fountain and past simple eatery Agriturismo La Rondinella. Next comes an amazing *torchio* (wine press) dated 1742, fashioned from a single chestnut tree. Go L here on Via per Trarego. It's not far to another fountain then a sign for n.10 for Trarego, a wide path heading NNW into chestnut woodland with some huge trees.

After a ruined house and a stream is a path junction where you keep R as per blue paint splashes. It quickly narrows and begins its zigzagging plunge down a steep wooded slope. At the bottom is heavy-duty steel netting close to the original **bridge** (548m) which crosses Rio di Cannero high over a dramatic ravine. Red/white waymarking takes over for the leisurely ascent on a good path via a sequence of terraces and stone huts in chestnut woods. A field edged by cherry trees is reached and a lane leads up to a path junction – go R on a minor road on the lower edge of **Trarego** (796m, 1hr 20min) with its neat gardens and cottages. ▶

For the village centre and café, fork left up any alley.

Keep on to the road intersection and bus stop.

A short distance R is the signed path junction where you fork R for Cannero. A lane leads through an arch and past a couple of houses to a gigantic chestnut tree. Then porticoed **Cappella della Vergella** marks the start of

Oggiogno is overshadowed by Cima di Morissolo

a lovely paved descent SE. It curves this way and that, with plenty of views to Cannero below and Luino on the opposite shore. Down at **Piancassone** you join the road from Trarego at a bus stop. A short way downhill fork R on a surfaced minor road with red/white waymarking, an older version of the road to Trarego. It concludes down at the main road near the bus stop at **Cannero Riviera** (197m, 1hr).

WALK 7

The Cannero–Cannobio Traverse

Start	Cannero Riviera ferry wharf
Finish	Cannobio ferry wharf
Distance	8.5km (5.3 miles)
Ascent/Descent	420m/420m
Difficulty	Grade 1–2
Walking time	2hr 20min
Access	Cannero Riviera and Cannobio are served by frequent VCO buses linking Verbania with Brissago. In both cases the bus stop is on the main road 5min from the lakefront, where ferries call in.

This justifiably popular walk links the two charming villages of Cannero Riviera and Cannobio, both set on the northwestern shore of Lago Maggiore, just short of the Swiss border. Easy lanes and paths leave walkers free to delight in the many belvederes over the lake. One highlight is beautiful car-free Carmine Superiore, founded in the 10th century as a fortress, and its stunning Romanesque church.

There are no refreshment points en route so be self-sufficient. The return trip to Cannero Riviera can be made by either bus or ferry.

From the ferry wharf at **Cannero Riviera** (197m) walk to the nearby northern end of the promenade and go L up Via Massimo d'Azeglio. Then it's R under an arch (sign for Nordic Walking), past a tiny harbour and up a stepped lane diagonally R between houses n.6 and 7 (while the Nordic walkers keep L). A jasmine-draped alley wanders by lush gardens and villas in enviable locations. The main road is crossed to a paved stepped way that climbs gently ENE to a leisurely panoramic level stretch touching on gardens, the odd house and swathes of chestnut wood.

Keep straight on at the hamlet of **Cheggio** (281m) to pass a house in a fantastically scenic location that takes in the curious 12–14th-century Castelli di

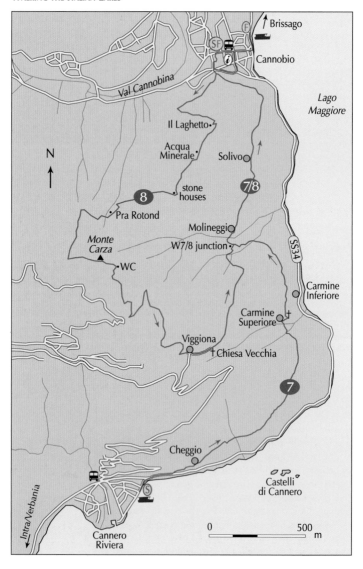

Cannero-cum-islands below. A wider paved track winds uphill into chestnut woodland where massive boulders dot the undergrowth. After a dried-up pond, ignore the turn-off for Carmine Inferiore and curve across a side stream to a stone bridge. Close by now is charming **Carmine Superiore** (305m, 1hr). Detour R or you'll miss the Chiesa di San Gottardo – what a gem!

The path climbs away from Cannero Riviera

> The tiny houses of Carmine Superiore, with old slab-tiled roofs, occupy a prominent rock outcrop overlooking the lake. Pride of place goes to the exquisitely frescoed Romanesque **Chiesa di San Gottardo**, dating from the 1300s, which has a welcoming terrace. The hamlet has but a handful of permanent residents who share the unique atmosphere with regular foreign visitors.

Follow the rocky alley-cum-high street down to a flight of steps and across a succession of streams. Touch on a road, then climb steps steadily uphill. ▶

As the way levels out look out for trenches amidst the trees, heritage of the Linea Cadorna (see Introduction).

65

Leaving Molineggi

After a waterfall comes the final climb that concludes at a **junction** (30min) with the path from Viggiona and Walk 8.

Turn R across the cascading stream and through **Molineggi** (454m) with its beautiful lake views and old water-powered mills, many of which are now holiday accommodation. Follow the lane in descent then go R on a signed path. A surfaced road is joined briefly, then follow signs L at **Solivo** on a lane through rural properties. Superb bird's-eye views of the photogenic Cannobio waterfront backed by the Swiss Alps are soon enjoyed. A path leads down to the residential area, where you are directed R. As you approach the main road, at a four-way intersection go L across the zebra crossing onto the alley Via A Giovanola. Fork R at the wash trough past pretty houses on Via Roma, which leads to Via M Giovanola. Branch R here past the shops and the Tourist Office to reach the bus stop on the main road at the church (220m, 50min).

For the ferries, proceed straight ahead on Via Umberto I to the lakeside, and go left for a host of inviting cafés not far from the ferry wharf.

WALK 8
Monte Carza

Start/Finish	Cannobio bus stop
Distance	17km (10.6 miles)
Ascent/Descent	900m/900m
Difficulty	Grade 2–3
Walking time	5hr
Access	Cannobio is served by frequent VCO buses linking Verbania with Brissago on the Swiss border. Many ferries also call in. The main bus stop is outside the principal church on the main road; the ferry wharf is 5min away on the lakefront.

A superb day out on Monte Carza, the easternmost extremity of the rugged mountainous ridge that delimits Val Cannobina and overlooks Lago Maggiore. Added historic interest comes in the shape of trenches belonging to the Linea Cadorna (see Introduction).

The walk follows old paved tracks and clear paths through beautiful woods en route to the summit belvedere, which arguably rates as the best on upper Lago Maggiore. The ascent is rather long but problem-free; the height gain puts many people off, and you will probably have the mountain to yourself. Only after Viggiona during the return will other walkers keep you company as a stretch is shared with the popular Cannero–Cannobio traverse (Walk 7). Take plenty of liquid refreshment and food as no cafés are encountered en route, but many hamlets during the descent have drinking fountains.

▶ From the bus stop outside the church at **Cannobio** (220m), turn S (in the direction of Verbania) along the main road (SS34, Via Uccelli). At the nearby intersection fork R at the sign for Val Cannobina. It's not far along to a clutch of signposts and a map board where you keep L then follow signs for Monte Carza, soon parting from the Viggiona/Cannero route. The road narrows quickly through houses and gardens, with views north to the village of Sant'Agata below Monte Giove. As the tarmac

See map for Walk 7.

comes to an end, a path breaks off L and begins a steady well-graded climb SW through woodland past derelict buildings. Further up you reach a lane and go R to where the path resumes. At the sign announcing **Il Laghetto** (little lake, 495m) – and with no water in sight! – branch L and soon rejoin the lane in ascent. Keep your eyes peeled for the many shortcuts.

At a field and farm signed **Acqua Minerale** (590m) ignore the detours for the impossible-to-find 'mineral water' spring. Ahead you encounter two stone houses at a path junction. Fork L away from the buildings through dense beech wood, but quickly veer R (WSW) and not far along you will be rewarded with a decent view down to Cannobio and the lake, thanks to the swathe of trees cleared for power lines. Further up a stream is crossed and the trees thin, opening up a vast panorama to the northern lake and Switzerland. Then you reach the summer farm **Pra Rotond** (940m, 2hr), set amid flower-filled meadows.

Now gird your loins for the final slog SSW. The path finally emerges on the upper ridge and a lane with a brilliant panorama. Go L for **Monte Carza** (1116m, 30min). The summit is a veritable carpet of broom and ferns, with wide-ranging views from Cannero to Luino on the opposite shore and the southern lake. ◄

For fantastic views north to Switzerland, make a short detour downhill left to the repeater aerial.

The path continues E to a rather old portable **WC** (!) sitting on the edge of the Linea Cadorna with a trench system. Turn sharp R here (SSE) to a chapel and panoramic picnic area. The red/white route soon forks L in common with a mountain bike (MTB) trail. Watch your step on the loose stones here. From bracken and heather the path moves down to a copse of silver birch. After a pylon, you leave the mountain bike route and fork R down through chestnut woodland to a concrete lane at the entrance to a property. Go L in descent to a fork (a short distance from a surfaced road), and L again along to a track intersection at a house – sharp R here sees you traverse a hollow thick with narcissus. Follow waymarks carefully SSE past old stone huts and huge chestnut trees and into the attractive village of **Viggiona** (693m, 1hr 10min). Clear signs point down an alley to Piazza Pasquale which encloses the Chiesa di San Maurizio, shady benches and cool drinking water.

Go diagonally L on Via per Cannobio, lined with stations of the cross. You soon pass to the L of a cemetery and exceptionally beautiful Romanesque **Chiesa Vecchia** that sports a vast slate roof. Now a paved way heads gently downhill through chestnut woods, past more trenches of the Linea Cadorna and to a strategic **junction** (30min) on the Cannero–Cannobio traverse.

Go L across the cascading stream and through **Molineggi** (454m) with its beautiful lake views and old water-powered mills, now converted into holiday accommodation. Follow the lane in descent then go R on a signed path. A surfaced road is joined briefly, then you're signed L at **Solivo** for a lane through rural properties. Superb bird's-eye views of the photogenic Cannobio waterfront backed by the Swiss Alps are enjoyed. A path now leads down to the residential area traversed at the walk start. Keep R for the main road and back to **Cannobio** and the bus stop (220m, 50min).

A jumble of rooftops at Viggiona

Chiesa Vecchia,
Viggiona

The most rewarding way to conclude this fantastic walk is to stagger down to the lakefront for well-deserved refreshment, while gazing back up to Monte Carza towering above the village.

WALK 9
Val Cannobina

Start	Orasso car park
Finish	Cannobio bus stop
Distance	20km (12.4 miles)
Ascent/Descent	700m/1150m
Difficulty	Grade 2
Walking time	5hr
Access	Orasso is served by sporadic VCO buses; you may need a taxi (Tel. 0323 71410, Mob. 348 7821699). **Note** Spoccia, 1hr along the way, has a morning bus so may be used as an alternative access (check which days it runs on). Cannobio is on the VCO bus line between Verbania and Brissago on the Swiss border. Many ferries call in here. The bus stop is outside the principal church on the main road; the ferry wharf is 5min away.

This absolutely wonderful full-day walk begins high up in Val Cannobina, 15km from Cannobio and Lago Maggiore. With the exception of a short stretch of tarmac between Gurrone and Cavaglio, it follows clear marked paths and paved lanes, crossing countless mountain torrents on elegant stone bridges and dropping in and out of the villages. The route is known as the Via Borromea for the pastoral visit of San Carlo Borromeo, archbishop of Milan in the 1500s, who travelled along it to visit his subjects.

The charming village of Orasso, set on lower Monte Torriggia, has the only grocery shop encountered today, alongside a café-restaurant. Cavaglio, a good three quarters of the way down, has the only other café. **Note** Every village on this walk has a tap or fountain with drinking water. There is accommodation at Orasso and Cavaglio (see Lago Maggiore Introduction).

▶ From the car park at the entrance to **Orasso** (700m) follow the red/white signs for Cannobio through the web of alleys past the ancient yet remarkably intact house Ca' du Vécc', with frescoes and a timber overhang. From the pretty church, its bell tower adorned with a sundial, is a superb view south to Monte Riga, dotted with stone

Orasso was named from the Latin oratio for 'prayer', and is the valley's oldest settlement, dating from the 1300s.

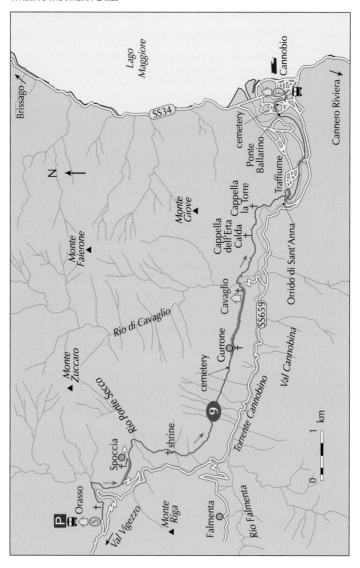

Spoccia and Orasso nestle in the woods in upper Val Cannobina

shepherds' huts. Heading NE the path narrows and enters wood on its way down to the first lovely bridge and stream crossing. A gentle climb leads S to a shrine and a road where you go uphill to a path junction, and L again up to **Spoccia** (798m, 1hr). All but deserted, this picturesque hamlet is brilliantly located. ▶

Return the same way to the road and turn L uphill past the 'H' helicopter pad to the junction R for Gurrone. It soon passes terraces with a row of stone huts and

From the war memorial look south towards Falmenta and Monte Riga; from the church gaze up to Monte Zuccaro.

VAL CANNOBINA

Val Cannobina is a rugged and densely wooded V-shaped valley, carved out by the eponymous torrent. Soaring above, the mountain fringes touch the 2000m mark. Their upper slopes are dotted with ancient alps, once summer pasture for livestock from traditional scattered villages, photogenic settlements of stone houses sporting tiny wooden balconies. In the face of limited opportunities for employment, and the downturn of the chestnut market due to competition from potatoes and cereals during the 19th and 20th centuries, the local population has dwindled from many thousands to just a handful today; for instance, Orasso shares a mere 120 residents with neighbouring Cursolo. Numbers do increase marginally in summer due to holidaymakers.

crosses Rio Ponte Secco. The ensuing lengthy stretch, due S and level, has sections cut into the rock face. A **shrine** doubles as a brilliant belvedere to Monte Zeda to the southwest, back to Orasso and Spoccia, Monte Zuccaro and the knobbly Gridoni outcrops, as well as Monte Riga and scattered hamlets. The next watercourse boasts a lovely waterfall and especially elegant stone bridge, and soon an orientation table puts names to all the mountains and villages far and wide.

Moving SE after a rocky point you pass two houses, then a water trough and a pasture clearing. Further on is a **cemetery** and path junction – keep L uphill to join the road into **Gurrone** (700m, 1hr 15min). ◄

It's worth taking time to explore this village, with its atmospheric covered passageways and wooden loggias.

The tarmac takes you through to the church and a car park, where a handkerchief corner of glittering Lago Maggiore is now visible. Now follow the unappealing steep road downhill ESE to **Cavaglio** (501m, 20min). Walk through the village, detouring to the bar/café if needed, as far as the church where drinking water is found at the foot of the bell tower. Soon you fork L where the old way resumes, an admirable piece of civil engineering as the mule track plunges in a succession of tight curves in easy descent to a majestic bridge high over Rio di Cavaglio.

The old way continues through shady woodland, soon forking L uphill to a stone column commemorating the fall of the mule bearing San Carlo in 1569. The path levels out en route to the **Cappella dell'Erta Calda**, fitted out with benches where wayfarers could rest. Val Cannobina has narrowed considerably now, and the descent soon begins in earnest, with plunging views to the riverbed below. At frescoed **Cappella la Torre**, now derelict, a toll would be exacted for the use of the road. You finally emerge on the road at **Traffiume**, and branch R to the dramatic ravine, the Orrido di Sant'Anna (250m, 1hr 30min) and its whitewashed church. The bridge here is said to date back to Roman times.

Take the stepped ramp down to the riverbed and pool, then follow the track for walkers and cyclists (*pista ciclopedonale*) E through the trees along the watercourse. After a road bridge keep on through fields to **Ponte Ballarino**.

This **bridge**, whose name means 'wobbly bridge', is a suspension bridge with a story to tell. In order to replace a precarious plank across the tumultuous stream (where people had been swept away), in 1933 villagers raised money themselves to finance a bridge. Flood damage later put paid to that one, and the current version was built in the 1980s.

Ponte Ballarino

Once on the opposite bank (café), walk straight ahead along the minor road to an intersection and branch R to pass the concrete wall of the **cemetery**. At the car park, keep R as per the sign 'Centro Storico'. An alley leads through to Piazza Casnago then Via A Giovanola where you turn L. Ahead stands the elegant bell tower not far from the main road and bus stop of **Cannobio** (220m, 1hr).

If you have any energy left, wander on down to the lakefront for a well-deserved drink.

En route to Gurrone

WALK 10
Cannobio–San Bartolomeo in Montibus Circuit

Start/Finish	Cannobio bus stop
Distance	12km (7.5 miles)
Ascent/Descent	450m/450m
Difficulty	Grade 2
Walking time	3hr 40min
Access	Cannobio is served by frequent VCO buses linking Verbania with Brissago on the Swiss border. Many ferries call in here. The bus stop at Cannobio is outside the principal church on the main road; the ferry wharf is 5min away on the lakefront.

An absolutely delightful circuit with masses of natural and historical interest. Highlights are the isolated Chiesa di San Bartolomeo in Montibus and the string of delightful old mountain hamlets and villages set in beautiful woodland on the eastern slopes of Monte Giove and Monte Faierone, close to the Swiss border. A dense web of paved tracks has linked them since time immemorial, and the many alpine streams are crossed via dozens of tiny arched stone bridges straight out of a fairy story.

Numerous variations are possible thanks to links with the main road and bus stops, such as at Darbedo and San Bartolomeo. There are no cafés or shops, but several villages have working drinking fountains.

From the bus stop at **Cannobio** (220m) follow the main road SS34 N to cross the bridge over Torrente Cannobino. Fork immediately L on the *pista ciclopedonale* (track for cyclists and walkers) past Albergo del Fiume and picnic benches. Take the first fork R through to the road; a short way L is a map and signposts for the beginning of the marked route at **Lignago** (20min). You puff up a steep cobbled ramp past houses to the path. Flanked by a wall smothered in honeysuckle that drenches the air with its perfume, the path moves off N, heading for woodland alive with birdsong. The first of the many dwarf stone bridges is soon encountered, a

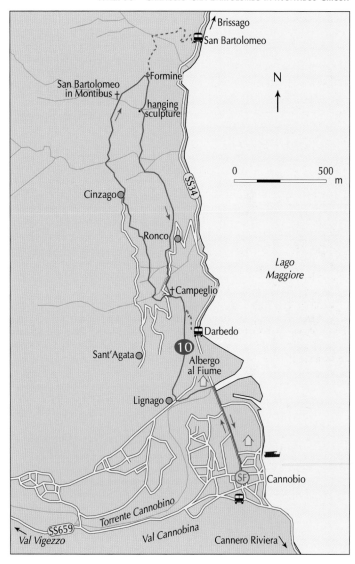

tad prior to a broad paved mule track from Darbedo on the main road.

> The excellent **network of paths** in this area served refugees and partisans during World War II. Stories abound of volunteers who put their lives at risk to help political and Jewish refugees, while there are tales of smugglers who exacted a stiff fee for their guiding.

Fork L here up to quiet **Campeglio** (351m, 20min) and its simple church. Waymarks point you up across the road; at a yellow house ignore the fork L for Sant'Agata and keep straight on a concreted lane. This transforms into a delightful wide woodland way in gentle ascent NNW across a sequence of stone bridges over cascading streams. At **Cinzago** (501m) you get a vast view over the northern reaches of Lago Maggiore to Locarno and Switzerland. The path wanders through the atmospheric village, almost a ghost town, with odd signs of renovation to the tall stone houses with their attractive wooden balconies.

It is possible to follow a signed path northeast to reach the main lakeside road at the village of San Bartolomeo for the bus back to Cannobio.

You're soon back in woodland on your way N to the ancient **Chiesa di San Bartolomeo in Montibus** (523m), where twin chestnut trees shade benches fashioned from mill stones. Now it's over another bridge and downhill via shrines to the close-packed jumble of stuccoed houses and well-kept vegetable gardens that comprise **Formine** (450m, 1hr 20min). ◀

At the tiny chapel, fork sharp R and thread your way down past houses, taking care not to miss the branch R (S). This quickly leads back into the wood as a level path, crossing a curious ravine and a pool with a hanging sculpture. The path narrows and swings in and out of side valleys, a short stretch of cable acting as a handrail where there is marginal exposure. It's a non-stop sequence of pretty green glens with bridges, streams and stepping-stones to **Ronco** (315m, 40min). This delightful village boasts gorgeous lake views, elegant flower-bedecked villas, a church, and a resident sculptor whose amusing

works are dotted around the alleys. Due S now it's past a goods lift and you join the road, turning R. Not far along you branch L through a car park and up to **Campeglio** (351m, 20min), past the church and up to the junction passed earlier on.

Turn L down the paved track and retrace your steps to **Lignago** and **Cannobio** (220m, 40min).

Old and new houses make up Campeglio

79

WALK 11
Monteviasco

Start/Finish	Curiglia
Distance	15.6km (9.7 miles)
Ascent/Descent	800m/800m
Difficulty	Grade 1–2
Walking time	4hr (3hr 10min cable-car option)
Access	Curiglia, 15km from the lakeside, can be reached on the Baldioli bus (Mon–Sat, line n.1) departing from Luino waterfront, a short stroll from the ferry wharf. Car owners should note that the road to Curiglia is particularly narrow and tortuous; park at the village or down at the cable car.

An age-old mule track consisting of well over 1000 stone steps ascends for almost 400m. And where does it lead? A place where time stands still: Monteviasco, a unique picturesque village, miles from the nearest road. It nestles in the alpine foothills of beautiful Val Veddasca, a pocket of Italian territory squeezed out of Switzerland. According to legend four deserters from an occupying Spanish army took refuge here in the 16th century and built homes. Desirous of company they successfully kidnapped some girls from Biegno on the other side of the valley. A delegation of furious men armed with pitchforks marched on Monteviasco but to no avail, as the victims were reportedly quite content to stay!

The walk commences with the marvellous mule track from Piero, near Curiglia – avoidable if you opt for the 10min cable-car ride to Monteviasco – and proceeds as a loop around the head of Val Viascola on clear paths and lanes. Curiglia has a grocery shop and café.

The funivia (cable car) timetable can be found at **www. monteviasco.it** under *orari*.

◀ From the bus stop below the church at **Curiglia** (666m) follow the *funivia* signs that take the L downhill fork of the road. It's possible to short-cut the first two bends in descent, then follow the tarmac NE along wooded Val Veddasca to the car park and cable car at **Piero** (549m, 30min). Immediately after the cables is the start (R) of the monumental mule track. A thousand or so perfectly graded steps climb due E up a wooded shoulder and past a handful of shrines. This is undeniably the most appropriate way to reach enchanting **Monteviasco** (926m, 1hr). The settlement looks west to the scattering of villages opposite, dotted over the steep wooded flanks of Val Veddasca below Monte Cadrigna, and a corner of Lago Maggiore can just be glimpsed.

MONTEVIASCO

While not exactly bursting at the seams with residents, the village seems to be doing notably better than similar alpine settlements that have road links, as it is inhabited year-round by 20 souls, and even has a twice-weekly doctor's surgery. In 1991 a cable car was built to serve the tenacious inhabitants and get the kids to school on time.

Nowadays this remarkable oasis is a magnet for visitors, the majority of whom go to dine at the modest family-run trattorias serving fresh local produce and traditional specialties. Rooms and dormitory accommodation are on offer at Rifugio Quatra Brighent (Tel. 0332 65811, Mob. 336 853493, info@valcuviaservizi.com www.itinerariesapori.it).

Walk through to the church and its belvedere terrace, and take the paved street L with red/white waymarks. Keep L at the next junction with an inviting rustic restaurant, and L again at a shrine, thus leaving the village. After a handful of working farms the path is less trodden and the surrounds wilder. Heading ESE you encounter pasture clearings, rapidly recolonised by bracken and broom once abandoned. Ignore a turn-off left for Alpe Corte and stick to the main path through copses of silver birch and a string of ruined huts, many of which have collapsed roofs. The path swings SE to cross two cascading streams amid forget-me-nots and alpenrose to reach the promontory of **Alpe Fontanella** (1081m), the highest point on the walk. Here are superb views over thickly wooded Val Viascola and beyond. Behind, northeast, a rugged wooded crest marks the border with Switzerland.

Handrails lead down to steps across two more cascading watercourses as you move to the southern side

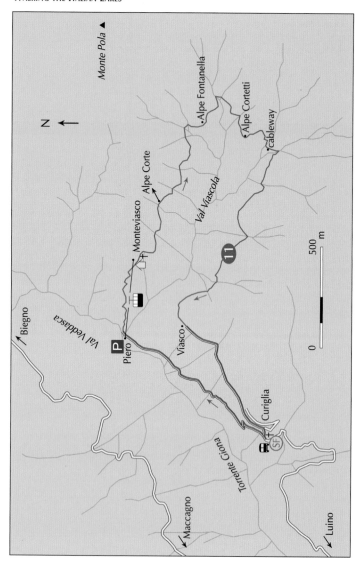

*The old way for
Monteviasco*

of the valley and begin a gentle climb SW to the saddle occupied by **Alpe Cortetti** (1048m, 1hr). The scattered buildings of this sizeable yet abandoned hamlet, nestling in divine rich green beech woodland, are immensely evocative. Not far downhill is the first of several fords, announced by a sign *guado*. In normal conditions the stepping-stones are sufficiently high, though after heavy rain you might get your boots wet. At the loading point for a rusty goods cableway and hut, the way widens to a level lane running WNW through gorgeous beech trees to a corner outcrop where Monteviasco can be admired.

Evidence of charcoal burning and woodcutting is clear en route to **Viasco** (873m), a cluster of dairy farms on a prominent corner. A surfaced road takes over for the rest of the way in descent SW to **Curiglia** (666m, 1hr 30min), and back to the bus stop.

WALK 12
Sasso del Ferro

Start	Laveno *funivia*
Finish	Laveno ferry wharf
Distance	8.5km (5.3 miles)
Ascent/Descent	110m/850m
Difficulty	Grade 2
Walking time	2hr (+ 20min for cable car)
Access	Laveno is linked to the opposite shore of Lago Maggiore by frequent vehicle and passenger ferry; it is also served by Ferrovia Nord trains on the line from Milano Cadorna. The *funivia* station is 5min from the ferry wharf – follow signs.

Standing out clearly on the central eastern shore of Lago Maggiore is imposing Sasso del Ferro, a mountain completely smothered in dark green woodland. Its great attraction is an old-style *funivia* cable car, more a *bidonvia* (rather like a string of metal buckets clanking their way upwards). It terminates at the 950m Poggio Sant'Elsa belvedere, easily one of the best on Lago Maggiore. The belvedere also doubles as a take-off platform for paragliders, and there's a popular café-restaurant. An optional extension goes to the 1062m top of Sasso del Ferro for a broader outlook over the hills of Varese.

The walk rates average in terms of interest; nearly all in descent, it spends most of its time in beautiful beech woodland, which rules out extensive views. It touches on Casere, a cluster of houses and a café/restaurant, then an old mule track and a quiet road descend to Laveno lakefront.

The panorama stretches from Monte Rosa across the vast lake and the islands, as well as down to Varese.

From the *funivia* station at **Laveno** (210m) enjoy the leisurely super-scenic ride through the trees to **Poggio Sant'Elsa** (950m) and awesome views. ◄

Instead of heading immediately downhill, from the gliders' launching pad, turn uphill through woodland on the steep red/white-marked path. A little way up, follow the disused ski lift that will lead you directly to the top of

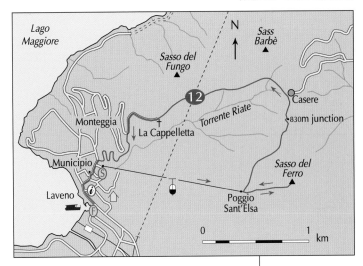

Sasso del Ferro (1062m), alive with swallows. Visibility permitting, the views here are 'limited' to the hills around Varese to the southeast, lower Lago Maggiore and the plains beyond.

Back down at Poggio Sant'Elsa (30min), take the path at the rear of the restaurant, signed for Laveno. It becomes a stony track running NNE through beech woodland, soon reaching a lane **junction** (830m, 30min) where you fork R. It's not far down to the saddle at Casere (750m). ▸

Turn off right here for the café-restaurant.

A wide mule track in excellent condition now begins its long descent W in mostly shady woodland high above the bed of Torrente Riate. Occasional clearings allow glimpses of the lake and Laveno below. At a shrine, **La Capelletta** (520m), are a couple of houses and a café.

Now the way is surfaced and quite steep at times. At the houses of **Monteggia** (at the sign for Brena), fork off the road onto a concreted lane. Later, tarmac takes over on a quiet but knee-testing road through a residential area. At a T-junction with pastel-stuccoed buildings, turn L along an old road with paving stones (Via Caprera) then

85

Laveno, overshadowed by Sasso del Ferro

R on Via Tinelli into Piazza Fontana and the Municipio palazzo. Here fork L on stepped Via Palestro, continue downhill towards the church and go L along the lakefront past the Tourist Office to the ferry wharf of **Laveno** (210m, 1hr).

LAGO DI COMO

Paved street at Naggio (Walk 17)

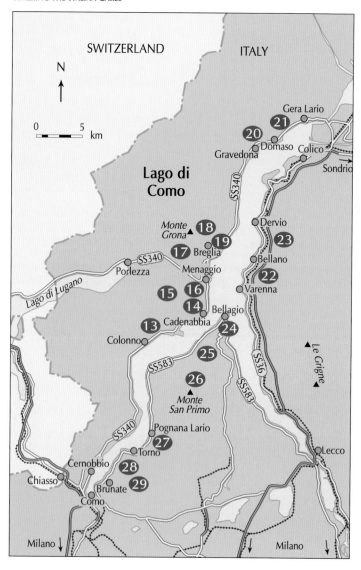

INTRODUCTION

How bless'd, delicious Scene! the eye that greets
Thy open beauties, or thy lone retreats;
Th' unwearied sweep of wood thy cliffs that scales,
The never-ending waters of thy vales.
William Wordsworth

'This lake exceeds anything I ever beheld in beauty, with the exception of the Arbutus Islands in Killarney. It is long and narrow, and has the appearance of a mighty river winding among the mountains and forests,' declared Shelley in 1818. Ever magnificent, the splendours of Lago di Como were also broadcast by the likes of Pliny and Strabone back in ancient Roman times. Today Italians inevitably associate it with the great writer Manzoni, whose landmark novel *I Promessi Sposi* (*The Betrothed*) begins there; the heroine Lucia shares her name with the traditional Lake Como rowing boat. Overseas visitors are attracted by the breathtaking scenery and romantic atmosphere, augmented by the host of villas and superb gardens – not to mention the glamour of international celebrities such as George Clooney, who has a home there.

Sala Comencina and the lower lake (Walk 13)

An upturned 'Y' in shape – rather like a tuning fork – the 146km^2 expanse of Lago di Como is wholly in Lombardia. It is fed mainly by the River Adda which flows in from broad Valtellina, recipient of glaciers and snowfields from the mighty Bernina and neighbouring Alps. And as it spreads southwards it is split into two branches by the spectacular Bellagio promontory. The Adda chooses the southeastern arm and leaves the lake at Lecco, flowing on to swell the waters of the River Po. Curiously there is no river exit at Como, at the end of the southwestern arm, so the town is vulnerable to flooding. These days it is rare to see the city barricaded against rising water, but back in the 1300s it was common, and blamed fairly and squarely on the Milanese Visconti dynasty, who constructed bridges at Lecco that substantially narrowed the watercourse, thereby obstructing flow.

The 17 routes described here will also show that the area has much to offer walkers. Lago di Como is strategically placed in relation to the Alps; trade routes known to the Celts and Etruscans between Switzerland and the southern plains logically intersected here, meaning that modern-day walkers often tread in centuries-old footsteps.

The Como–Brunate funicular (Walks 28 and 29)

EXPLORING THE LAKE

In the south **Como**, the centre for the Italian silk industry, is a convenient and especially lovely place to stay. Its pedestrian-only centre is graced by an exquisite Romanesque cathedral and a host of outdoor eateries and cafés on the water's edge (Tourist Office Tel. 031 269712, www.lakecomo.it). Stay at good value Hotel Quarcino (Tel. 031 303934, www.hotelquarcino. it) or Hotel Posta (Tel. 031 266012, www.hotelposta.net). Good ferry services commence here. Como has two railway stations: located 5min uphill from the waterfront is San Giovanni-Como for the main line from Milano Centrale that continues via Chivasso into Switzerland. The other belongs to the Ferrovie Nord, and is located close to the lake's edge; this runs to Milano Nord Cadorna where there are Metro connections to Milano Centrale. ASF buses start out at Como to serve the lake's western shore: all stops to Menaggio and then to Colico at the head of the lake.

One of Como's great attractions is the marvellous funicular railway constructed in 1894. Walks 28 and 29 begin with the ride. It still trundles almost vertically to the hill retreat of **Brunate**, where the wealthy would escape the summer heat of the plains in the privacy of elegant villas surrounded by shady pine and beech woods. It is still a nice place to stay and doubles as a superb lookout for admiring Torino and the Monviso on a clear day. Sleep at Vista Lago (Tel. 031 364070, www.albergovistalago. it) or at Albergo Paradiso (Tel. 031 364099, www.paradisosullago.eu) at San Maurizio (on Walk 29).

From Como the narrow road SS583 hugs the eastern shore on its way to Bellagio, served by an ASF bus. It passes through a string of picturesque waterside villages, including **Torno**, the conclusion of Walk 28, then **Pognana Lario** where Walk 27 begins. High above towers the vast Triangolo Lariano, the mountainous peninsula separating the Lecco and Como arms of the lake, perfectly triangular in shape (as the name implies). It is dotted with glacial erratics, huge rock chunks broken off distant mountain flanks where the glacier once flowed, and carried for miles to be deposited far from their original geological context. Several can be admired during Walk 27.

The northernmost tip hosts picture-perfect, world-famous **Bellagio**, bang in the middle of the lake, beautifully located on a promontory that divides Lago di Como in two – its name means 'two lakes'. And Punta Spartivento, its northernmost extremity, 'divides the wind' that comes rushing down from the Alps. The town attracts a chic 'want-to-be-seen' crowd who come in the hope of spotting the rich and famous in sleek motor launches or lounging in luxuriant villa gardens. Hype apart, it is a wonderful place to spend any length of time, but be aware that accommodation and restaurants do not fall into the budget category (Tourist Office Tel. 031 951555, www.promobellagio.it).

Bellagio has excellent passenger and car ferry links with Varenna on the eastern shore and Menaggio to

The wonderful gardens of Villa Carlotta look across the lake to Bellagio (Walk 13)

Villa 'La Quiete' at Bolvedro near Tremezzo (Walk 13)

the west. Lecco Trasporti runs buses to and from Lecco; for taxis Tel. 335 6299588. Walk 24 explores the surrounds of Bellagio, Walk 25 from nearby Guggiate aims for the Monte Nuvolone lookout, while Walk 26 climbs to superb Monte San Primo, the highest point on the Triangolo Lariano. Accommodation possibilities include Hotel Europa (Tel. 031 950471, www.hoteleuropabellagio. it), Bellagio B&B (Tel. 031 951680, www.bellagiobedandbreakfast.com) and Hotel Centrale (Tel. 031 951940, www.hc-bellagio.com). At nearby Pescallo is Hotel La Pergola (Tel. 031 950263, www.lapergolabellagio.it).

From Como the SS340 heads along the western shore via **Cernobbio** with its outstanding villas. Lakeside **Colonno** marks the start of

Walk 13, the 'Greenway' that wanders parallel to the road all the way to Tremezzo and adjacent **Cadenabbia**. Here stands Villa Carlotta with lemon arbours and luxuriant beds of gorgeous rhododendrons (www.villacarlotta.it). It has frequent ferries, and grand hotels lining the waterfront. Walk 14 begins from nearby Griante.

Unpretentious **Menaggio** is perfectly located for walks on the western lake and is a good place for an extended stay to explore the surrounds thanks to excellent public transport on both land and water (Tourist Office Tel. 0344 32924, www.menaggio. com). Frequent passenger ferries call in from Bellagio and Como, as does the Varenna car ferry. ASF buses on the Como–Colico line are frequent, and local runs start out here. It has a good range of accommodation, including Ostello La Primula (Youth Hostel: Tel. 0344 32356, www.lake-comohostel.com), waterfront Albergo Bellavista (Tel. 0344 32136, www.hotel-bellavista.org) and Hotel Garni Corona (Tel. 0344 32006, www.hotel-garnicorona.com). Away from the lakeside at Loveno is Hotel Loveno (Tel. 034432110, www.hotelloveno.it), transit point for Walk 17 that climbs into Val Sanagra. Continuing a fair way uphill is the quiet village of **Breglia**, the start of Walk 18 which aims for Monte Grona and the neighbouring panoramic ridge, along with Walk 19 to the village sanctuary. A good bus service from Menaggio comes this far, and you can stay at Albergo Breglia (Tel. 0344 37250, www.breglia.it).

On the SS340 road west for **Porlezza** on the Lago di Lugano is Croce with Hotel Adler (Tel. 0344 32171, www.hotel-adler-menaggio.it), a key landmark for the start of Walks 15 and 16.

Although the mountain slopes are gentler along the shoreline of the upper western edge of the lake, the backdrop of the dramatic alpine line-up is more impressive. Visitors to this part of Lago di Como are fewer in number, so it's a quieter area to visit. Moreover it has been dubbed the 'Little Tuscany of Lario' due to a wealth of exquisite Romanesque churches, exemplified by landmark black-and-white chequered Santa Maria del Tiglio on the lakefront at **Gravedona**. Served by ASF buses and

At Menaggio (Walk 17)

Lucias: traditional lake boats

ferries, this is the first town of interest to walkers and Walk 20 begins here, giving a good taste of this pretty district. Stay at Hotel La Villa (Tel. 0344 89017, www.hotel-la-villa.com) or Hotel Regina (Tel. 0344 89446 www. reginahotels.it). Gravedona has a lakefront Tourist Office (Tel. 0344 85005 turismo.gravedona@gmail.com).

Buses and ferries continue around to lakefront **Domaso** and the beginning of Walk 21 (Tourist Office Tel. 0344 96322, www.promodomaso.com). Rooms are available at Ristorante dei Pescatori (Tel. 0344 96088, www.ristorantedeipescatori. com) and Hotel Camping Europa (Tel. 0344 96044, www.hotelcampingeuropa.com), which doubles as a well-organised campsite.

It's only a short bus ride to the resort village of **Gera Lario** where Walk 21 concludes, close to the mouth of the River Mera in an area beloved of windsurfers. Across Pian di Spagna the lake shore curves south to the huge River Adda and the town of **Colico**, at the entrance to broad Valtellina. From here two roads run south, the coast-hugging SS72 and the SS36 which speeds through tunnels. In parallel from Colico is a handy railway line (from Sondrio), stopping at all stations en route to Lecco then on to Milano Centrale. Important stops include quiet **Dervio**, where the occasional ferry also pulls in, and where Walk 23 terminates. The village is set on a sizeable alluvial promontory formed by debris carried by the River Varrone.

Next comes **Bellano**, once dubbed the 'little Manchester of Lario' for its wool and cotton mills, most of which stand empty and forlorn today. Its modern-day claim to fame is an awesome *orrido* ravine touched on in Walks 22 and 23. To its south and set high above the lake is the little-visited location of Santuario di Lezzeno (on Walk 23) with B&B del Viandante (Tel. 339 4626859, www.bebviandante. com).

The vital mid-lake car ferry from Menaggio docks at laid-back **Varenna**, a good alternative base for visiting Lago di Como without the crowds often encountered on the western shore. Stay at lovely lakeside Hotel Olivedo (Tel. 0341 830115, www.olivedo.it) and stroll along the charming waterfront past well-tended gardens and pretty pastel-coloured houses and villas. Walk 22 begins here.

MAPS

The Kompass 1:50,000 map n.91 Lago di Como covers all the walks and is adequate for planning, but the large scale precludes much detail. An excellent 1:25,000 *carta dei sentieri* (walking map) for the Triangolo Lariano and Walks 24–29 is available free of charge at local Tourist Offices or www.triangololariano.it. For Walks 14–19 around Menaggio request the Comunità Montana 'Alpi Lepontine' 1:25,000 *carta topografica escursionistica* at the Tourist Office. They also have a simplified map downloadable from their website www. menaggio.com, as does the Bellagio Information Office on www.promobellagio.it. The upper lake (Walks 20 and 21) is covered by the 1:35,000 map Alto Lario Occidentale published by the Comunità Montana Alto Lario Occidentale, and on sale in the immediate area.

TRANSPORT

- ASF buses
  Tel. 031 247111
  www.asfautolinee.it
- Como–Brunate funicular
  Tel. 031 303608
  www.funicolarecomo.it
- Ferrovie Nord
  Tel. 800 500005
  www.ferrovienord.it
- Ferry timetables
  Tel. 800 551801
  www.navlaghi.it
- Italian State Trains
  Tel. 892021
  www.trenitalia.com
- Lecco Trasporti buses
  Tel. 0341 359911
  www.lineelecco.it

WALK 13

Colonno to Cadenabbia on the Greenway

Start	Colonno, Bar Sport
Finish	Cadenabbia car park
Distance	10.5km (6.5 miles)
Ascent/Descent	100m/100m
Difficulty	Grade 1
Walking time	3hr 15min
Access	The C10 bus line (ASF) along the northwestern shore of Lago di Como calls in at Colonno – alight at the central bus stop outside Bar Sport. Cadenabbia is also served by the C10 bus line, as well as ferries.

Never straying far from the divine lakeside, the leisurely 'Greenway' drops in and out of the villages tucked off the main road (negligible ascent/descent). Several sections of the ancient Via Regina transalpine way are incorporated in the route, which is a combination of walkers-only lanes and paths and occasional surfaced roads. Buses and ferries call in at most of the lakeside villages, so you can do selected chunks and come and go at pleasure. Around halfway, peaceful Lenno has a smattering of waterfront eateries and cafés, though plenty more are encountered en route.

Steel lozenges embedded into the path show the way, as do blue/yellow arrows set at most key junctions. **Note** The official start (*inizio percorso*) of the Greenway is at the southernmost end of the village of Colonno, and to reach it entails a nerve-racking walk along a narrow stretch of busy main road. It is more logical and pleasant to begin the walk in the middle of the village, as described here.

From the bus stop at Bar Sport in **Colonno** (200m) – with an eye out for passing traffic – walk in the direction of Como to cross the bridged stream. Close by is Bar Marisa where you go down the steps below road level. Then turn immediately L up the alley to a path T-junction. Here are blue/yellow arrows for the Greenway, so go R. This leads through the fascinating old part of the village then gently

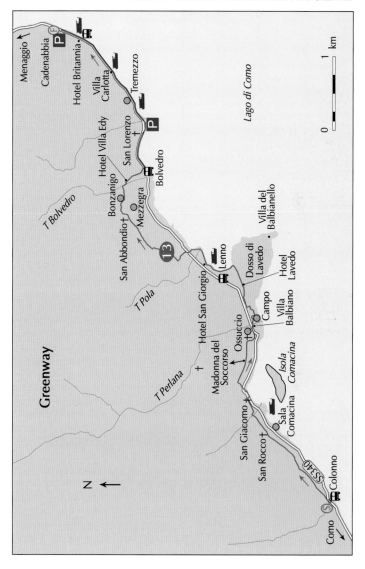

97

ascends through vegetable gardens and orchards, flanked by stone walls. Isola Comacina comes into sight on the lake below, with an inspiring mountainous backdrop.

Ignore the fork R passaggio al lago unless you need the village of Sala Comacina.

A level stretch goes above a newer residential area and a cemetery and past the yellow shrine of **San Rocco**, recognisable by the painting inside of the saint with a wound on his leg. ◀

A delightful cobbled lane descends gently amidst olive and fig trees to the main road, which you need to cross for the tiny 12th-century Romanesque **Chiesa di San Giacomo** (40min): a pretty spot.

Continue on the path parallel to but below the road, then branch L on a pedestrian crossing and up steps past Osteria del Giuanin. Ignore the route for the sanctuary Madonna del Soccorso and fork R here along the tarmac to a square between the local school and a park. Proceed straight across at a roundabout and not far on turn R down Via Castelli to another admirable Romanesque church. Keep L of the building to reach the war memorial and bus stop on the road at **Ossuccio** (30min).

Cross over to Piazza Cardinale where you can peek through a railing to see stately **Villa Balbiano** with its ornate gardens. A pedestrian bridge leads over a river (Torrente Perlana) and into the atmospheric photogenic centre of **Campo**, once an ancient Roman settlement. Arrows point the way along its maze of alleys, past Villa Monastero, and back up to the road. It's not far to a caravan park and, further on, **Hotel Lavedo**. Continue in the same direction along the edge of a park with picnic tables, the inland edge of the wooded promontory **Dosso di Lavedo** which belongs to Villa Balbianello (Tel. 0344 56110 www.fondoambiente.it), out of sight from here, but well worth a visit.

The lovely lakeside awaits, as you curve around to **Lenno** (30min), with inviting alfresco cafés and restaurants, not to mention a bus stop on main road. Past the ferry landing stage stick to the lakefront past Hotel San Giorgio and onto a shingle beach. At its end, an alley heads up to cross the road to a flight of steep steps. Turning R, it's onto a quiet road through a new residential area which enjoys

vast views over Lago di Como. Just 5min along, keep diagonally L on cobbled Via Pola Vecchia and then Via G Brentano Mezzegra, with a chapel. After the huge rococo **Chiesa di San Abbondio** which stands out like a beacon and has lovely views to the Bellagio peninsula, you head downhill to the Municipio of Mezzegra, which occupies an elegantly ornate palazzo. An alley leads through the charming old village and a covered passageway below 17th-century Palazzo Rosati in **Bonzanigo** (270m).

San Giacomo stands on the lakeside

With a great outlook east to the Grigne mountain range, fork down the tarmac way, lined with olive trees. Then go L along Via delle Gere, over a stream, R downhill and then L past **Hotel Villa Edy**. A paved alley leads down to the main road at **Bolvedro** and a bus stop (50min).

A promenade L along the water's edge passes marvellous stately Villa La Quiete, then the **Chiesa di San Lorenzo**. Go R and duck into the beautiful grounds of

Along the waterfront at Lenno

The vicinity of traffic along this section tends to encourage walkers to bail out earlier.

the civic park on the lakefront with aged shady trees and a fountain. It's a popular spot for picnics and even swimming.

It's not far now along the pavement past the ferry wharf of **Tremezzo** to superb **Villa Carlotta** and its magnificent stepped gardens, a must-visit (Tel. 0344 40405 www.villacarlotta.it). The Greenway proceeds through **Cadenabbia** (201m) past the magnificent façades of grand hotels, another ferry wharf and bus stop opposite Hotel Britannia, before coming to its official conclusion after the minuscule Lido beach, at a car park (45min). ◀

WALK 14
San Martino Circuit

Start/Finish	Cadenabbia (Griante), Hotel Britannia
Distance	5.7km (3.5 miles)
Ascent/Descent	250m/250m
Difficulty	Grade 1–2
Walking time	3hr
Access	Cadenabbia can be reached by ferry; from the wharf, turn right along the road to Hotel Britannia. Otherwise catch a C10 bus (ASF) and get off opposite the hotel.

This delightful circuit leads to the little church and sanctuary of San Martino that clings to the sheer cliff face high over the lake: a peaceful spot where visitors can drink in a far-reaching panorama and enjoy the tranquillity. The church is of great symbolic importance to the local population as it is home to a precious 15th-century statue of the Virgin and Child that miraculously found its way up here, ostensibly without human help! The paved path leading up to the church is lined with shrines and votive statues, and is both steep and stepped but not difficult.

The return path loops through woodland and passes rural properties before joining the quiet road that descends to the bustling lakeside.

From **Hotel Britannia** at **Cadenabbia** (201m), turn away from the lake on Via Roma. Only minutes up at a church, take the flight of steps (Via Mazzini) up to a road where you turn R again past the **Municipio** (Town Hall), then L as you reach the **war memorial**. This street (Via Brentano) passes a park before curving R to a T-junction at a yellow house with a ceramic Madonna and child. Branch R under an arched passageway and proceed along the alley (Via Tommaso Grossi) through the old district to reach Piazza **San Rocco** and its church. Keep R here as per signs for the 'Chiesa San Martino', soon bearing L on tarmac.

You quickly reach the signed fork R for steps down to a **bridge** across a stream. Heading essentially NW the path, lined with vegetable gardens, follows the stream. Soon begins a long series of paved and stepped ramps climbing endlessly through pretty woodland. Votive shrines are dotted along the way, and there's a small chapel too – all a good excuse to get your breath back!

At a path junction with a *Caduta Massi* (rockfall) warning sign, fork R around a gully on a lovely rock path with a handrail NE for the last panoramic leg to the **Chiesa di San Martino** (475m, 1hr 30min): a simply stupendous spot. The building appears to be clinging to the cliff edge – needless to say there are breathtaking views over the lake. A shady picnic area invites walkers to enjoy the place.

Return to the path junction and take the fork R. This lovely high path, with far-reaching views, narrows a little

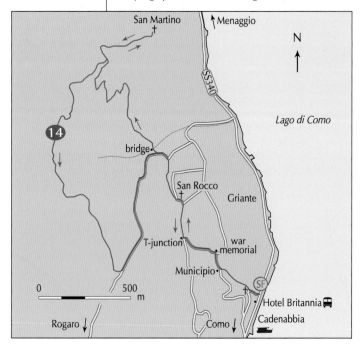

and bears S with a stretch of handrail, before dipping past summer farms. Further on it leaves the wood and heads SE as a lane to join the Rogaro–Griante road (1hr). Turn L here and downhill to pick up Via San Martino once more. Then retrace your steps for the final 30min back to **Cadenabbia** (201m, 30min) on the lakeside.

San Martino perches high above the lake

WALK 15
The Bocchetta di Nava Traverse

Start	Croce, Hotel Adler
Finish	Cadenabbia bus stop
Distance	9km (5.6 miles)
Ascent/Descent	500m/685m
Difficulty	Grade 2
Walking time	3hr 15min (+ 1hr 30min extension)
Access	From Menaggio take bus C12 for the short trip up to Croce; the bus stop is opposite Hotel Adler. A C10 bus (ASF) or ferry can be used for the return to Menaggio.

A lovely walk up through woods and pasture beneath towering peaks. The return meanders downhill on an old military track across carpets of sun-drenched Mediterranean flora accompanied by simply magnificent lake views.

Towards the end, an optional and highly recommended detour can be made to the wonderful belvedere of San Martino (see Walk 14); either way the day concludes on the lovely waterfront at Cadenabbia, part of Griante. Drinking water and a picnic should be carried as nothing reliable is found en route.

From the bus stop and **Hotel Adler** at **Croce** (392m) turn R along the road past the church, and follow signs for 'Golf', which entails forking L up Via A Wyatt. At the old wash trough fork R as per red/white waymarking for n.2, Via dei Monti Lariani. After a concrete-based lane, bear R onto a grass ramp and up across the road to a flight of steps. A delightful sunken way climbs for a while through shady deciduous woodland. At a minor road, go L uphill and around a corner to the immaculate whitewashed chapel **Madonna delle Grazie di Paullo**.

Here turn L on the gravel lane, Via ai Monti di Nava, past houses scattered here and there in pretty wood-land and fields. The way continues straight through **Miè**

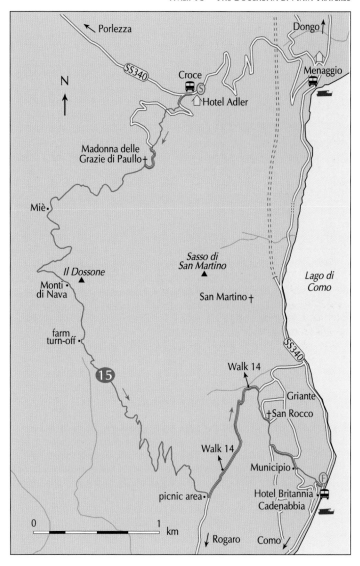

(685m), a cluster of modest buildings and a signpost at an intersection of lanes. Hazelnut and chestnut trees are common, succeeded by beech as you ascend. Marked regularly with red/white paint splashes, the lane veers SE in constant ascent, coming out at last near the meadows and summer houses of **Monti di Nava** (885m, 1hr 30min), overshadowed by massive Monte Crocione.

Stay on the lane as it heads S in gentle descent past a modest **farm** where an arrow points you L off the lane/n.2 and into the cover of woodland. Soon a series of tight zigzags indicate that this was once a military road, though it gives way to a rougher stony path bearing L (SE) across limestone mountain flanks with superb views over the lake and the peninsula with Bellagio. This is a simply beautiful descent route. Below is Griante, an assemblage of villas and gardens, while closer at hand to the north the precipitous outcrop of Sasso di San Martino with its tiny landmark church stands out. Back in woodland again, ignore a fork R for the Cappella degli Alpini, then keep L at the ensuing junction. This finally reaches rural properties then a picnic area with a drinking fountain next to a minor road from Rogaro (1hr 15min). Turn L and follow this road.

A few minutes along is the signed turn-off for **San Martino** should you have the desire and energy to make the lovely detour – slot into Walk 14, allow an extra 1hr 30min and be prepared to follow the description in reverse.

The road heads downhill (N) to veer R as Via San Martino, passing a lower turn-off for San Martino. Stick to this street as it goes R as a pedestrian way past houses to the **Chiesa di San Rocco**. Now it's R again on Via Tomaso Grossi, an alley through the residential area and up to an arched passageway underneath a house. At the tarmac and a yellow house with a ceramic Madonna and child, turn L on Via Brentano past a park and a bar to the war memorial. Go R past the **Municipio** (Town Hall) and soon L on steps (Via Mazzini) which leads down to Via Roma

whence the main lakeside road in the vicinity of Hotel Britannia at Cadenabbia (200m, 30min).

The ferry wharf is a short distance to the R, while the bus stop to return to Menaggio is immediately opposite.

Monti di Nava and the Crocione

WALK 16
Crocetta

Start/Finish	Croce, Hotel Adler
Distance	3.5km (2.2 miles)
Ascent/Descent	110m/110m
Difficulty	Grade 1
Walking time	1hr
Access	From Menaggio take bus C12 for the short trip up to Croce; the bus stop is opposite Hotel Adler. **Note** It is possible to drive as far as the termination of Via GB Pigato where you can park.

It takes very little effort to get to the Crocetta, 'little cross', for a beautiful bird's-eye view over the township of Menaggio along with inspiring vistas up and down the lake. A further bonus is the chance to explore a web of trenches that snake through the trees high above the lake shore. Belonging to the Linea Cadorna, they date back to 1912–16 when Italy feared invasion (see Introduction).

This is an easy short walk that begins on a quiet surfaced road and moves onto lanes in shady woodland, good for stretching your legs in preparation for longer outings.

From the bus stop at **Croce** (392m) turn R along the road past the church, and follow signs for 'Golf', which entails forking L up Via A Wyatt. You pass an old washing trough still gushing water and ignore the path L where Walk 15 branches off. Even from here the lake views are lovely!

Not long after a hairpin bend in the road you fork L on Via GB Pigato. The last of the houses is soon passed and you enter the woodland on a shady lane. Nearby is a sign and the start of the shelters and **trench system** belonging to the Linea Cadorna – take some time out to explore.

Then resume the lane for a short uphill stretch to a fenced clearing with chestnut trees and a hut. Branch L

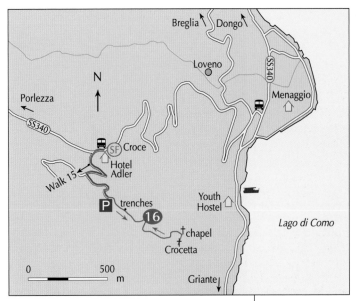

Gorgeous views over Menaggio and the northern lake

109

A trench near Crocetta

Close at hand is Monte Grona (north), while to the northeast the light grey peaks of the Lepontine rise at the head of the lake. The rugged Grigne stand out due east.

here to find more historic trenches and then the Capella degli Alpini **chapel** in a stunning spot overlooking Menaggio and Lago di Como. ◄

Near the chapel an arrow on a tree points through the wood SSW on a clear path to where the wooden cross **Crocetta** (40min, 502m) stands on the breathtaking edge of a cliff. The view from here is dominated by the Bellagio promontory and the lovely Lecco branch of the lake.

Retrace your steps back to the bus stop at **Croce** (392m, 20min).

WALK 17
Val Sanagra

Start/Finish	Menaggio, Piazza Garibaldi
Distance	14km (8.7 miles)
Ascent/Descent	550m/550m
Difficulty	Grade 2
Walking time	5hr 20min
Access	Menaggio has excellent ferry and bus links. The walk start is located close to the lakefront, in the pedestrian-only zone. Local Menaggio buses serve Naggio and Codogna on the return. **Note** It is possible to drive as far as Piamuro, where there is a small car park.

A wonderful long and varied outing, experiencing old cobbled mule tracks, scattered mountain hamlets and summer pastures, a dramatic cascading river, water-powered mills, pretty villages and woodland, as well as elegant villas and charming homes in Menaggio and nearby Loveno, where, from the late 1800s, patrician families would spend their vacations.

After climbing up from the lakeside through quiet residential areas dotted with stately villas, the walk enters the Val Sanagra. Good signed paths cross ravines on stone bridges to reach summer pastures and long-established hamlets. Note that the paths in the uppermost valley are little frequented and can be a little overgrown (check at the Menaggio Tourist Office if in doubt). The return follows the west side of the valley, taking in pretty villages – Naggio is outstanding – with some stretches on quiet farm roads. Take a picnic unless you plan on lunching at the Mulino Chioderia (Tel. 0344 30152).

From waterfront Piazza Garibaldi at **Menaggio** (202m) take pedestrian Via Calvi up to the main road; duck L then immediately R around the church and proceed along Via Caronti. Turn R up pedestrianised Via Leoni and soon L on cobbled Via Castellino da Castello, which incorporates the remains of medieval castle walls. Lovingly tended gardens and pretty villas punctuate the uphill

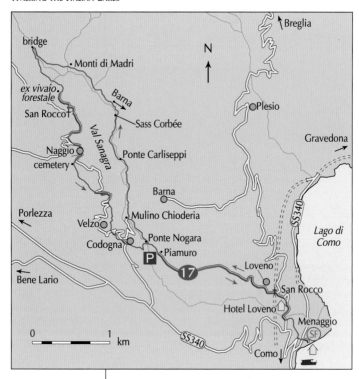

stretch, along with inspiring lake views. When you reach the road for Plesio, turn R across the modest Sanagra river to **Hotel Loveno** and a bus stop, where you fork L up a flight of steps.

Another short stretch of road will see you at the shrine to **San Rocco**; go L past a clutch of signposts and into quiet **Loveno**. Through Piazza Milius veer R uphill past old residences and beautiful villas. At a war memorial go L to follow the road, skirting the parkland of Hotel Royal and past the baroque façade of San Lorenzo church near Villa Vigoni. Now yellow/black signs point you L rather steeply up the tarmac way, to conclude the surfaced section at a cemetery and car park at **Piamuro**

(374m, 50min), as well as the entrance to the Parco della Val Sanagra.

Branch L (NNW) on the lane marked n.4 across a flat meadow edged with woodland at the foot of Monte Grona. This bears NW through farmland and over a rise with a shrine. It's not far downhill to the first of a series of photogenic bridges, **Ponte Nogara** (393m) over the Sanagra. However, the path keeps to the pretty right bank, past a tinkling cascade and a stretch of stream popular with dippers. Not far along, after an old furnace, is another lovely bridge close to the **Mulino Chioderia** (412m, 30min), once a mill and water-powered nail

Bridge near Mulino Chioderia

113

factory, now a trout farm and country-style restaurant. Keep R on the lane past the fish troughs and into the narrowing river valley. Derelict mills dot the peaceful shady way. Ignore the forks for Barna, and continue to a tiny hamlet and mill and elegant stone bridge – **Ponte Carliseppi** (456m) – where you cross to the L bank.

The path on the ensuing stretch is a little rough due to flooding in 2009 and follows the river, wilder here, closely. At a dramatic ravine with lovely pools and a massive limestone overhang, a new footbridge crosses to the R bank. The path, narrow but clear and marked red/white, soon reaches a huge boulder apparently blocking the valley. This is **Sass Corbée**. Steps cut into the rock aided by a handrail lead upwards. The red/white-marked path weaves its way in and out of fallen rocks, gradually gaining height in woodland dotted with gorgeous cyclamens. The going is cool and shady, and may be slippery.

Not far up a wider path (from Barna) is joined at an old limekiln, Forno della Calce. Go L (NW) here as the

Ponte Nogara

going levels out between old drystone walls, high above the river. Several clearings and minor side streams are traversed and huddles of simple houses, long abandoned, bear witness to the erstwhile settlements and life in Val Sanagra. The path is occasionally messy where the stream has overflowed, finally emerging on to a lovely peaceful pasture subject to the inexorable invasion of brambles. This is **Monti di Madri** (570m, 1hr 15min).

A faint path follows the watercourse upstream for about 10min to a timber **bridge** (640m) which you cross. On the opposite bank a narrow but clear path veers L past another small limekiln and joins a wider rough track. This climbs steadily SW to a field and the **ex vivaio forestale** (former forestry nursery, 701m). The track is now surfaced and continues through dense woodland with the occasional glimpse to Monte Grona (northwest) not to mention the wild valley below. At the chapel of **San Rocco** (761m, drinking water) turn L on a quiet road. Not far down, fork L on a lovely stepped way, then resume the road to a second shortcut which leads straight into the cool alleyways and tiny squares of the charming old village of **Naggio** (657m, 1hr).

Down in Piazza San Antonio walk past the front of the eponymous church and bus stop, ignoring the road sign for Menaggio, and through to the **cemetery**. Here is a sign for the 'Strada Vecchia per Codogna' (the old road for Codogna), a shady grassy lane that heads S. Further on, it shares a couple of bends with the road, then (where a path forks L for Vecchia Chioderia – ignore) the mule track resumes S through fields, with the bonus of lake views. The actual village of Velzo is bypassed, and you cross the road once more in the vicinity of a huge church. Ahead now rise the magnificent Grigne beyond Lake Como. The track drops to nearby **Codogna** (450m) and elegant Villa Camozzi. Only metres below is the start of a delightful cobbled way signed for **Piamuro**. Once through the houses, it winds its way down to **Ponte Nogara** (393m, 1hr) encountered on the outward route.

Now retrace your steps back to **Piamuro** (15min), then on to **Loveno** and **Menaggio** (220m, 40min).

WALK 18

Rifugio Menaggio and Monte Grona

Start/Finish	Breglia
Distance	9km (5.6 miles)
Ascent/Descent	950m/950m
Difficulty	Grade 2+
Walking time	4hr 40min (+ 1hr/1hr 30min extensions)
Access	From Menaggio take bus C13 to Breglia. By car, drive up the winding road to the village, then proceed on narrow Via ai Monti di Breglia to the parking area at Monti di Breglia, saving 1hr 40min.

This absolutely superb walk on the steep mountainous flanks of Monte Grona, immediately to the rear of the lakeside village of Menaggio, makes a memorable day outing. Clear paths traverse pasture, woodland and open grassland to an elongated crest with spectacular views to the spread of the Alps as well as over beautiful Lago di Como. Lengthy uphill sections are tackled in the outgoing section, so go prepared and fit. A hospitable mountain refuge, Rifugio Menaggio, is visited, handy for lunch or refreshments, or an overnight stay.

One extension leads to the summit of Monte Grona: note that this is rather narrow and tricky in spots, so a head for heights and sure footedness are essential (Grade 3). A second easier extension climbs to the Bregagnino.

The laid-back rural village of Breglia (see Walk 19), perched dizzily above the lake, has a handy hotel and café/ restaurant – Albergo Breglia – close to the bus stop.

◄ From the bus stop opposite the cemetery at **Breglia** (748m) turn L up Via ai Monti di Breglia, heading mostly N. A short distance uphill, after a water trough on a corner, fork R for the path marked red/white that avoids the tarmac. It shortcuts through woodland, crosses the road and continues uphill past a house. When it emerges on the road near a cableway, turn R for a short stretch, then after a watercourse the path resumes uphill via houses and meadows.

After a further road crossing a steep and possibly muddy path leads through old chestnut terraces past

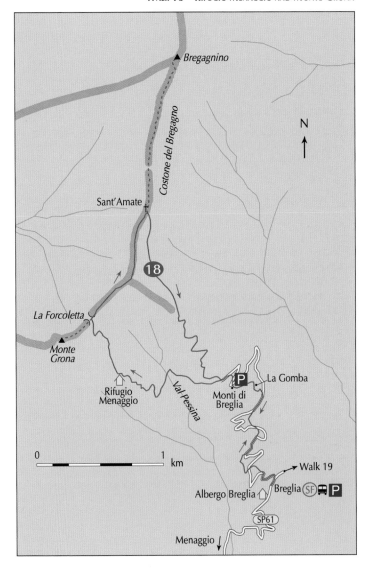

ruined stone houses. **Note** A short way up, ignore arrows pointing right, and keep straight ahead. Lined with bushes of fragrant broom, the way soon rejoins the road, bearing R to a fountain and picnic tables with great views. A signed path now points you L to a concrete/stone ramp past **La Gomba**. Steps through a wood of silver birch and ferns lead to a picnic table and the parking area at **Monti di Breglia** (1085m, 1hr).

A matter of minutes uphill, the way forks: turn L for the Sentiero Basso, initially W along a lane. Approaching Val Pessina this narrows, soon beginning a steep zigzag climb into hazel woods. ◄

The cableway for the refuge ahead runs overhead, though lengths of cable occasionally lie across the path – watch your step.

It will be with great satisfaction that you emerge from the cover of trees to the clearing with **Rifugio Menaggio** (1383m, 1hr) and its drinking fountain (open mid-June to mid-September and most weekends, Tel. 0344 37282 www.rifugiomenaggio.eu). The refuge has stunning views towards Lecco and the rugged Grigne to the east, without forgetting the lake. Refreshments and meals are on offer.

At the rear of the building fork uphill, following the signs for Monte Grona 'via normale'. Wasting no time, the clear if narrow path gains height over stony ground to the saddle of **La Forcoletta** (1627m, 45min), in the company of huge black crows and swallows. For Monte Grona take the following route, but be aware that it rates Grade 3 on difficulty.

Extension to Monte Grona (1hr return)

Turn L (SW) up a shoulder that quickly becomes steep and exposed, demanding some hands-on scrambling. It leads gradually below the main ridge, finally gaining the summit of **Monte Grona** (1730m, 30min) with amazing views that even take in the Matterhorn. Take special care on the steep descent on loose stones back to **La Forcoletta**.

Turn R (NE) on the clear path along the broad grassy crest, Costone del Bregagno. A thrilling glimpse of glaciated Monte Rosa to the west is enjoyed, along with a sweep of the lake beyond Bellagio and down as far as Lecco. The

grey Grigne stand out to the east, while at the head of the lake are the Lepontine Alps with Monte Disgrazia. The undulating pasture has colourful patches of purple-blue gentians, heather and pretty pink alpenrose. The next landmark, the modest chapel of **Sant'Amate** (1617m, 15min), also offers a beautiful outlook northwest to Lago di Lugano. For even vaster views, consider the following extension, a straightforward route up a broad crest.

A scenic pause during the ascent to Monte Grona

Extension to Breganino (1hr 30min return)

In common with the VML route – Via dei Monti Lariani – take the well-worn path marked in red/white for the steady 300m ascent due N. Pauses to get your breath back will come in useful to enjoy the ever-improving views. The **Bregagnino** (1902m, 1hr) is a lookout *par excellence* over the upper lake and the vast spread of the Lepontine Alps, with ice and snow-capped peaks galore. Return to **Sant'Amate** (1617m, 30min) the way you came.

For the descent, take the signed path SSE, a diagonal traverse of a spectacular mountainside with dizzying

The broad grassy crest leading to Sant'Amate

lake views. It drops past a repeater aerial where Rifugio Menaggio can be seen. Down in woodland once more, ignore turn-offs and finally pass the Sentiero Basso fork, before reaching **Monti di Breglia** again (1085m, 1hr 10min).

Unless you're lucky enough to bag a lift, the rest of the descent to **Breglia** (748m, 40min) is the same as the outward route.

WALK 19

San Domenico and the Santuario di Breglia

Start/Finish	Breglia
Distance	3km (1.8 miles)
Ascent/Descent	60m/60m
Difficulty	Grade 1
Walking time	1hr 15min
Access	Bus C13 from Menaggio goes to Breglia; it is feasible to drive up and there's a spacious car park at the village entrance.

High above Menaggio and the lake, this is a pleasant easy stroll through beautiful chestnut woodland. It circles the 865m Motto outcrop, chosen by local inhabitants for both a sanctuary and a tiny shrine on the dizzying cliff edge, with expansive views across Lago di Como. The sanctuary dates back to 1781, and houses a revered statue of the Madonna sculpted in marble.

The tranquil village of Breglia is located on a broad saddle well below the forbidding ridge of Monte Grona-Bregagnino, and has a friendly café-hotel-restaurant near the walk start.

Breglia has been a place of transit for centuries. There is a Roman tomb (6th century ad) opposite the bus stop; burials were placed at the roadside so as to keep the memory of the dead alive, and a road ran through Breglia en route to a trans-alpine crossing. The village name derives from the Celtic for 'bridge' or 'passage'.

From the bus stop at **Breglia** (748m) walk across to the car park. In the far R corner take the lane that leads into woodland, and keep L at the fork soon encountered. Initially on a level, it starts a gentle climb SE past some beautiful aged chestnut trees and remnants of man-made terraces from the times when chestnuts were part of the staple diet locally.

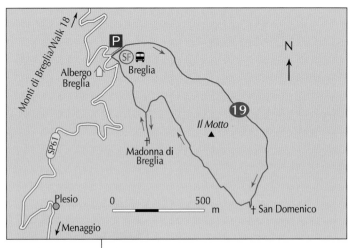

The sanctuary offers fantastic views over the lake

En route through gaps in the foliage you are tempted with sparkling views of the vast lake below, but you have to wait until the tiny chapel of **San Domenico** (800m) for the breathtaking ones, undeniably worth waiting for! But do watch your step on the rocks here.

The lane continues NW around the mountain. At a pasture clearing turn L and soon go L again to join the broad cobbled stepped way (aka Via Crucis) lined with the mini shrines of the stations of the cross. On a prominent outcrop, the white church known as the **Santuario della Madonna di Breglia** (770m) offers yet more wonderful views.

Once you've had your fill of panoramas, go back down the stepped way and keep straight on. This will bring you down to houses, concluding at the bus stop at **Breglia** (748m, 1hr 15min).

WALK 20
Gravedona to Domaso

Start	Gravedona ferry wharf
Finish	Domaso ferry wharf
Distance	4km (2.5 miles)
Ascent/Descent	200m/200m
Difficulty	Grade 1–2
Walking time	1hr 30min
Access	Gravedona and Domaso are served by hydrofoil and ferry services and bus line C10.

This appealing walk wanders through quiet hamlets and vineyards high above the northwestern shore of the lake, well away from crowds. The paths and lanes are not waymarked, but with a little attention to these directions walkers won't have any problems. Be aware of the presence of steep flights of steps – worthy of the vertical Amalfi Coast! A longish stretch of surfaced road is followed on the middle section, but it is only used by locals.

Domaso is a lovely spot for lunch at a lakeside café or restaurant. Its historic heart, with narrow alleyways and elegant buildings, also merits a visit.

Don't miss the graceful chequered black-and-white 12th-century Romanesque **Chiesa di Santa Maria del Tiglio**, on the waterfront a short stroll south from Gravedona ferry wharf, past the Tourist Office. Another point of interest is the home of the great scientist Alessandro Volta (of electrical fame), native of Gravedona, passed early in the walk.

▸ From the ferry wharf at **Gravedona** (201m) go R (N) along the waterfront to **Piazza Mazzini**. Turn L here (at a sign for Ristorante Ca' de' Matt) through to Via al Castello where you go R then L up Via G Dentore. This leads through a square, where you continue on Via San Rocco to the main road.

The route can be linked with Walk 21 from Domaso to Gera Lario.

123

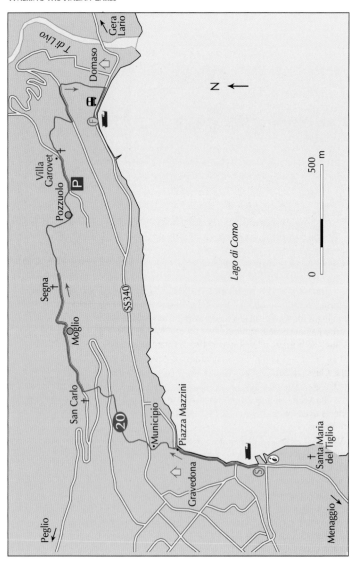

Houses set high above the lake

Turn R past the **Municipio** and a sign for Volta's house, and soon L up the alley Via Dossi e Segna, soon forking R for Via Pessina. A lovely way, it passes beneath a road and proceeds quite steeply up to a fork at a new house with huge gates. Go L to the road and continue straight up past houses. This concludes in the vicinity of the **Chiesa di San Carlo** (350m, 30min), where swallows make good use of the tower.

Turn R (E) on the narrow surfaced road to enjoy great views over the northern curve of the lake and wooded promontories. Below is the Gravedona power station. After the houses of **Moglio** comes the final climb, to the rural settlement of **Segna** (395m), complete with a tiny church, San Lorenzo. Walk through to the last of the modest houses and a wash trough, where the road reverts to a lane, passing well-kept vegetable gardens. The unusual outlook from here takes in the mouth of the Adda river where it empties into Lago di Como at Colico, the different coloured waters of river and lake providing dramatic contrast.

125

Old drinking fountain at Pozzuolo

A short way along (about 100m) fork R (E) off the lane on a small path between stone walls. This makes its way diagonally downhill through vineyards and cultivated terraces flanked by woodland and into the charming hamlet of **Pozzuolo** (310m). Among its delightful features are a cool fountain and trough used by the locals to chill their drinks.

◀ Down at Piazza Acone and a car park, follow the tarmac the short distance to a shrine opposite **Villa Garovet** and branch R onto a lovely stepped lane. Leading downhill it reaches houses. Where the steps end, keep L on a pedestrian way across a stream on a level, then R down to Piazza Feloy Leonardo and a car park. Now follow the sign for Ristorante La Contrada through a district distinguished by elegant houses.

It's worth making a short detour right to the church and benches for enjoying lake views.

You emerge on the main road and waterfront of **Domaso** (201m), where benches shaded by Stone Pine trees overlook a pebble beach with a view back to Gravedona and its landmark church. Inviting cafés and eateries are dotted along the waterfront. Turn R for the ferry wharf or the bus stop.

WALK 21
Domaso to Gera Lario

Start	Domaso ferry wharf
Finish	Gera Lario bus stop
Distance	7.5km (4.6 miles)
Ascent/Descent	280m/280m
Difficulty	Grade 2
Walking time	2hr 20min
Access	Domaso is served by hydrofoil and ferry services and bus line C10. From Gera Lario take the C10 bus as no ferries call in.

Located on the quiet top northwestern shore of Lago di Como, Domaso has a charming historic centre. From the lakefront the route climbs through woodland to a succession of photogenic villages of age-old stone houses and narrow alleyways; Aurogna is particularly attractive. En route are wonderful sweeping views of the northern corner of Lago di Como, its water dyed different hues of blue and milky grey by the Adda and Mera rivers that empty their load of glacial debris and earth into the basin. Gera Lariois a very popular spot for windsurfers thanks to the strong breezes that prevail at the top of the lake.

▶ From the ferry wharf at **Domaso** (201m) walk along the lakeside promenade in the direction of Colico, as far as the bus stop at Piazza Ghislanzoni Oreste and its cafés. Fork diagonally R along the alleyway, Via Regina. This leads via an arched passageway through to Piazza Feloy and onto the imposing 18th-century **Chiesa di San Bartolomeo**. Walk past the entrance and take the road signed for Gaggio/Pozzolo, though you soon leave it for a narrow way across a stone bridge over the River Livo. A stepped cobbled way now leads upwards to a chapel dedicated to San Silvestro, where you keep L, passing houses and pretty gardens. There are lovely views over to Colico and the mouth of the River Adda.

At the road, take the path signed for **Madonna delle Nevi**, not far off. The church was erected in the 1600s

This route is a logical continuation of Walk 20 between Gravedona and Domaso.

Approaching Valle Vercana

in memory of victims of a plague that swept the district. Here the path enters a short rock tunnel bored into the mountainside, then climbs to a road where the restored stepped track branches R. Further up this goes R to cross a stream, ascending to **Arbosto** (354m, 45min) with its war memorial, square and Chiesa di San Salvatore.

Turn R along the road past Ristorante Bellavista. After a café-tobacconist, ignore Via Arbosto then branch L up a cobbled lane that heads uphill past orchards. After crossing a road it enters woodland interspersed with fields, climbing steadily and flanked by stone walls and patches of nettles. Ignore the fork near a shrine. At a road near modern terraced apartments, turn R to where a lane coasts through woodland and passes a picnic table. A gentle ascent NE touches on pasture and abandoned stone houses, along with excellent views to the Mera and Adda rivers with their backdrop of the light grey peaks of the Alps edging on Valtellina. Through flourishing chestnut woodland the way narrows to a path and drops into Valle Vercana, past a tiny stone **molino** (mill).

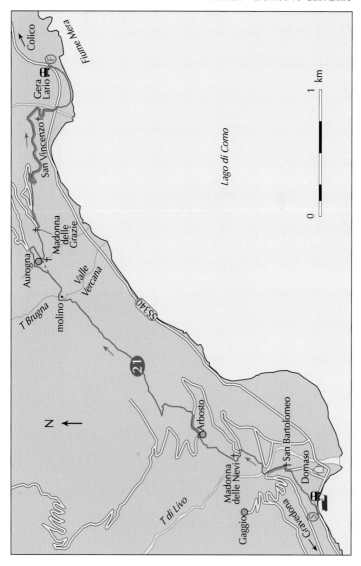

After crossing the cascading Brugna torrent, the path emerges into cultivated fields and widens. As the lane begins to descend towards asphalt and power lines, branch L onto a path past an old building and through well-kept vegetable gardens (or see the shortcut below). A footbridge across a stream leads straight into the beautiful old hamlet of **Aurogna** (420m, 45min). Continue in the same direction past the Municipio. Not far on, at a building featuring a modest Madonna fresco (house n.7), turn sharp R downhill out of the village to meet tarmac, and R again to a new flight of steps down to a shrine.

Old stone houses in Aurogna

*Church of San
Vincenzo*

Shortcut to bypass Aurogna
If for some reason you're in a hurry, instead of branching L towards the village, stick to the lane as it crosses a stream and fork immediately R on new steps to the shrine and the main route.

Veer L across the meadow to where the old way and stone wall resumes through mixed woodland, as well as plenty of walnut trees and grape vines. Soon after the **Chiesa di Madonna delle Grazie** comes a short stretch of tarmac (SP2). It's not far to a junction where you keep L to drop under the road for a path past houses. The road is joined again briefly to the solemn grey **Chiesa di San Vincenzo** that dates back to the 1400s.

Cross over the main road and go L across the river to take the cycleway down to the lovely lakeside, complete with a marina and hub for windsurfers. At the car park and café, turn L for the main road and bus stop in **Gera Lario** (200m, 50min).

WALK 22

Sentiero del Viandante 1: Varenna to Bellano

Start	Varenna ferry wharf
Finish	Bellano railway station
Distance	6.2km (3.8 miles)
Ascent/Descent	270m/265m
Difficulty	Grade 2
Walking time	2hr 45min (+ 30min extension)
Access	Varenna is reached by frequent ferry runs from Bellagio and Menaggio, and has trains on the Lecco–Sondrio line; station 5min from the waterfront. Bellano has fewer boat services so it's easier to catch the train back to Varenna.

The middle section of the lovely eastern shore of Lago di Como is a great deal quieter than the western shores. This walk rambles through woodland and charming old hamlets, using a stretch of the multi-day Sentiero del Viandante. The 'wayfarers' route' links Abbadia Lariana (north of Lecco) with Colico at the top of the lake.

Generally speaking waymarking and signposts are fairly frequent – the Sentiero del Viandante abbreviated as SdV or SV – though extra attention is needed to avoid missing key turns. This Varenna–Bellano leg tends to be better trodden and signed than latter sections. Whereas cafés and restaurants en route are rare as hens' teeth, scenic lunch spots are in good supply so take a picnic and plenty of drinking water. The villages of Varenna and Bellano have lovely lakefront promenades and cafés where a well-deserved drink can be enjoyed.

This walk can be linked with Walk 23. The suitable place to slot in is San Rocco in upper Bellano.

◀ From the ferry wharf at **Varenna** (220m), to the R of Hotel Olivedo and alongside a signboard for the Sentiero del Viandante, go up the stepped way Via alla Riva. This crosses a road and continues up cobbled Via della Croce, winding past houses and into woodland to the village of **Vezio** and a path junction (350m, 30min). Here an interesting detour takes in the modest castle as follows.

Side trip to the Castello di Vezio (30min return + visit)
Go R past the church and onto the prominent outcrop with olive trees where the castle (www.castellovezio.it) stands presiding over Varenna. It comes complete with falconry demos and a snack bar. Return to the path junction afterwards.

A ferry pulls in at Varenna

Turn L (E) at the junction down a steepish paved path to an old bridge spanning Torrente Esino, thick with wild mint bushes. Up the other side to a road where you do a quick dogleg L then R, past a small factory and through to the lovely baroque chapel of Madonna di Campallo with its cypress trees, graceful archway and frescoed interior. With lovely lake views, the path curves happily along through olive groves and up to the village of **Regolo** (320m, 30min), with Piazzetta Bassa and the Chiesa di San Giovanni Battista.

Here you veer L on Via degli Orti, uphill to cross a road and continue on a shady way lined with high stone walls. This emerges on a minor road, where a new housing development has unfortunately cancelled a stretch of the old track. So turn R up the tarmac through an old

133

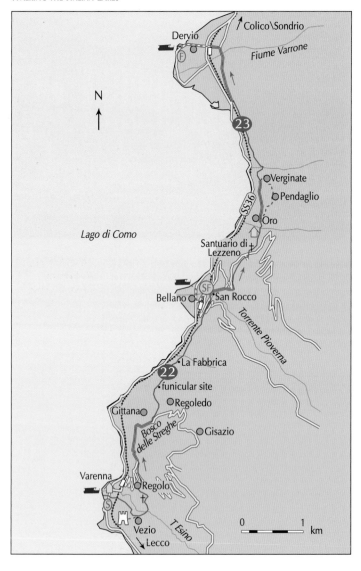

quarry, past a shrine on a corner and down to a nearby intersection. Here the Sentiero del Viandante resumes as a shady lane through the **Bosco delle Streghe** (witches' wood!) and across a stream. Where the trees thin out you can see down to the village of Gittana clustered around its church. Keep straight ahead, ignoring turn-offs to hamlets and a fork for Gisazio.

The walk-through Madonna di Campallo shrine

> Near the Gisazio fork the Sentiero del Viandante crosses a man-made ravine that once featured a remarkable piece of engineering – a hydraulic-powered **funicular** ran up here from 1903 until the 1950s, transporting passengers to the erstwhile spa resort at Regoledo above.

The peaceful way proceeds NE between drystone walls and looks down to Bellano and the upper spread of the lake. The next landmark is **La Fabbrica**, an elegant, traditionally designed house dating back 300 years and long used as an inn for wayfarers. A 1732 stone council boundary marker is soon reached, and picnic tables should you feel the need for a rest. A bridge is crossed;

The path starts descending towards Bellano

To continue along Walk 23 to Dervio, pick up the directions from this point.

then begins the gentle descent towards Bellano, high above houses and the railway station. An extensive block of long-abandoned factories stretches out towards the waterfront. The outlook also takes in the Dervio peninsula further to the N. You cross a road and turn R for a couple of metres to where the path resumes as a paved way to where Torrente Pioverna flows through a dramatic *orrido* (ravine) many dizzy metres underneath. Over a bridge stands the white **Chiesa di San Rocco** (240m, 1hr 15min). ◄

Turn L down the stepped way Via San Rocco. Soon at a gate on the L is the entrance to the awesome *orrido*. Continue down to Piazza San Giorgio in **Bellano** (206m). Keep L to the main road, and L again across the Pioverna. The railway station (30min) is along the fourth street on the L. For the ferry wharf, from Piazza San Giorgo keep R and through the old town to the lakeside.

WALK 23
Sentiero del Viandante 2: Bellano to Dervio

Start	Bellano railway station
Finish	Dervio railway station
Distance	6.2km (3.8 miles)
Ascent/Descent	170m/135m
Difficulty	Grade 2
Walking time	2hr 45min (+ 30min extension)
Access	Bellano and Dervio are easily reached by trains on the Lecco–Sondrio line, but have infrequent ferry services.

This rewarding route along the eastern edge of Lake Como uses a stretch of the Sentiero del Viandante, the old 'wayfarers' route'. While not as straightforward as the Varenna–Bellano leg (Walk 22), this section does have fairly frequent waymarking and signposts, but keep your eyes peeled so as not to miss key turns. There's little in the way of cafés or restaurants but the abundance of panoramic lunch spots make up for that, so go prepared.

A recommended if steep variant extension is given to the hamlet of Pendaglio, a veritable eyrie, accessible only by foot. The cluster of traditional mountain houses no longer has any permanent inhabitants, just a handful of people seeking peace and quiet who spend weekends and summers here.

Near the walk start is the entrance to Bellano's famous *orrido*, where for a modest fee visitors can wander along suspended walkways to admire the dramatic **ravine of the Torrente Pioverna** as it crashes towards Lake Como. If you strike lucky and find it open, take time out for a visit.

▶ From the railway station at **Bellano** (206m) follow the main road N across the bridge over Torrente Pioverna. Take the first R – Via Roma – past an old cotton mill and through to Piazza San Giorgio. At the church on the corner, fork R on the stepped way and past the gated

See map for Walk 22.

entrance for visits to the awesome *orrido*. Keep on up to the white landmark **Chiesa di San Rocco** (240m, 30min).

Continue upwards on Via Ombriaco past the cemetery. The lane climbs long and steadily, under a road and past blocks of flats. It finally reaches a signed junction at a wash trough and forks L along a concrete alley through a new residential zone. Proceeding NNE it crosses the road twice en route to the huge cream-coloured 18th-century **Santuario di Lezzeno** (370m, 30min) and a quiet hamlet. Turn L around the building to the marvellous lake belvedere; Monte Grona and the Bregagnino stand out on the western shore directly opposite.

A turn R along a signed alley leads past B&B del Viandante and through a charming cluster of old houses. The route touches on the road (in the vicinity of a bus stop) with a clear view to the Dervio peninsula. A gentle uphill path is followed, another road crossed again and a lovely lengthy cobbled section ensues, threading its way past tiny farms and fields where fig, walnut and cherry trees abound. A downhill leg runs parallel to the road before traversing a ravine alive with crashing cascades and past a ruined mill building.

Not far on, at a house, where the variant for Pendaglio breaks off (see below), go L downhill to the road towards the village of **Oro** (279m). Turn R along the asphalt (for approx 2km) and past rural properties, keeping R at a fork and uphill. Follow this a little further until it is joined by

San Rocco above Bellano

Verginate is visited on the walk variant

a narrow concreted track (from Verginate) where a signed turn-off proceeds straight ahead (as a path now).

Variant via Pendaglio (30min extra)
Keep R uphill on the paved lane which soon resumes as an old stepped way, climbing through woodland once more, up, up and up. At last you emerge at **Pendaglio** (480m, 30min). In a world of its own, it consists of a whitewashed church alongside age-old stone houses with ancient timber balconies. Go L at the church for a narrow path that plunges to tiny picturesque **Verginate** and its car park. A concreted lane drops quickly via a couple of curves to a signed turn-off R, where you resume the official Sentiero del Viandante.

A well-signed and lovely level section, cobbled in parts, heads N through woodland and fields with views towards Dervio and its promontory. Gentle descent leads through chestnut woodland and down across a watercourse. A short climb leads past rock flanks overlooking the railway line and warehouses. Finally, steps lead down to the road – go R along Via Duca d'Aosta and cross the Fiume Varrone, which was responsible for forming the peninsula occupied by the town. Soon go L on Via XX Settembre (the fourth street on the L) to the railway station at **Dervio** (238m, 1hr 45min). For the ferry wharf, continue towards the waterfront for another 10min.

WALK 24

Around Bellagio

Start/Finish	Bellagio ferry piers
Distance	6km (3.7 miles)
Ascent/Descent	85m/85m
Difficulty	Grade 1
Walking time	2hr
Access	Frequent ferries visit Bellagio from ports on the western shore of Lake Como, as well as the car ferry from Varenna on the eastern bank; it can be reached by bus from Como and Lecco.

An easy stroll around the beautiful surrounds of the lakeside town of Bellagio, justifiably renowned for its spectacular location on a dramatic mountainous promontory in the middle of the lake. Old paved ways pass through perfectly terraced gardens, olive groves, fishing hamlets and stately villas set in vast parkland. The walk is a good introduction to this central part of Lago di Como as villages on both sides of the headland are visited, and you can see across the water to where rugged ridges dwarf far-off settlements.

While the route appears initially rather short, it will mysteriously stretch out to occupy at least half a day as myriad detours beckon, or even longer if you stop off at the gardens of Villa Melzi, not to mention take time out for a leisurely lunch – restaurants are to be found at Pescallo, San Giovanni and Loppia.

From the lakefront and ferry piers at **Bellagio** (202m), opposite the Tourist Office start up the stepped alley Salita Mella between boutiques and restaurants. At the top is bustling Via Garibaldi. It's worth making the brief detour L to the square hosting the main church; in the top R corner is a photogenic medieval watchtower, now a second Tourist Office.

Resume Via Garibaldi L (S) past shops and restaurants to where the Municipio stands alongside the

Salita Mella at the beginning of the walk

tiny 11th-century Chiesa di San Giorgio – you need the stepped way opposite, L, signed for Nuovo Hotel Miralago. Walk gently uphill at first, between walled gardens and over a rise. The alley heads downhill towards the water, branching R past pretty flower-decked houses to the peaceful waterfront of **Pescallo** (199m). As the name suggests, it was once an important fishing village, with its own market. Relax on a bench to drink in the panorama taking in the Lecco arm of the lake backed by the light grey Grigne range of mountains. Nearby is Piazza del Porto with Hotel/Ristorante La Pergola. Take the road, Via Pescallo, gently uphill past a nursery to the **cemetery** where many foreign residents have been laid to rest.

Here, at the crossroads, turn L on the pavement of Via Valassina alongside long-established olive groves which give this district its name: Oliveiro. Soon historic greenhouses mark the start of the remarkable property of **Villa Giulia**.

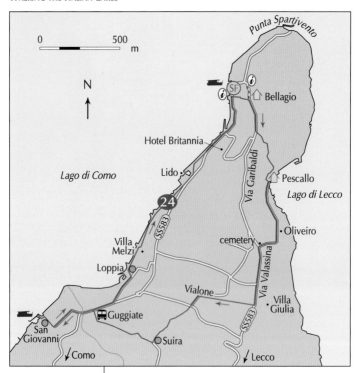

Originally dating back to 1624, **Villa Giulia** was completely overhauled and redesigned in the late 1700s by Count Pietro Venini and renamed to honour his wife. He had a huge swathe of land flattened in front of the building and fashioned into a broad avenue so as to grace the villa with access and views to both branches of the lake.

So turn R now onto this curious '**Vialone**'-cum-vast meadow with an amazing outlook west to the Crocione crest high over Griante. Don't go all the way to the far end, but fork L on the first minor road you reach. Then cross over Via Volta and take the cobbled way (Via

Taronico) straight ahead past houses. This becomes a stepped path, gently progressing uphill with impressive views back northwest to Monte Grona and Menaggio standing out against a backdrop of the upper lake.

The tiny square of **Suira** (282m) is reached, surrounded by elegant dwellings. Turn R here for the pedestrian alley Via Monumento, flanked by high walls and gardens. A short way downhill, keep L on Via La Derta, a lovely if steepish descent to an old villa and Piazza Sant'Andrea at **Guggiate** (209m).

A café and bus stop are located on the main road where you turn L with care. Not far along, after a river crossing, fork R onto a quiet road amidst parkland into charming **San Giovanni** (203m) with its fascinating museum of instruments for navigation (Tel. 031 950309 www.bellagiomuseo.com). Turn R down Via Pescatori to the lakeside and ferry wharf, directly opposite Villa Carlotta and the spread of Cadenabbia on the opposite shore.

Retrace your steps to **Guggiate** and continue on for a matter of minutes before forking L down to the tiny waterfront hamlet of **Loppia** (197m), once home to fishermen. It is here that the tree-lined Vialone concludes with steps down to an ornamental gate. On the waterside, don't miss the elegant traditional lake rowing boats and massive old gondolas used until the late 1900s for transporting goods and livestock. After a restaurant is the entrance to **Villa Melzi**, well worth the modest entrance fee for the relaxing lakefront pathway and a wander around the spectacular beds of rhododendrons and camellias in the beautiful English-style garden (www.giardinidivil-lamelzi.it). Otherwise detour the gardens via the road, watching out for traffic.

The conclusion of the Vialone near Loppia

The two routes join up at the far end of the Melzi property, passing the once-grand **Lido** to the lakefront promenade where flourishing flowerbeds and giant bushes of rosemary are interspersed with benches, perfect for drinking in the glorious uplake panorama in the company of ducks and cormorants. Past the monumental old **Hotel Britannia**, long empty, to arrive back at the ferry piers of **Bellagio**.

WALK 25

Belvedere del Monte Nuvolone

Start	Guggiate bus stop
Finish	Ristorante La Baita bus stop, Parco San Primo
Distance	14km (8.7 miles)
Ascent/Descent	1130m/240m
Difficulty	Grade 2
Walking time	4hr 15min
Access	Guggiate is a short bus trip south from Bellagio on the C30 line; the C36 bus serves Parco San Primo throughout the summer months – check the timetable for return runs. Both are managed by ASF.

This is a protracted climb on old paved mule tracks and good paths to a wonderful belvedere over Lago di Como. The mountain's name is a reference to 'large cloud', but try and time your visit for a clear day, for instance immediately after stormy weather, when the views north will stretch all the way to the snow-capped Alps. En route are many great viewpoints, but all are eclipsed by the breathtaking panorama that awaits at the top. The Belvedere del Nuvolone is not the actual peak, as this is shrouded in trees, but a perch on the northernmost extremity of a thickly wooded ridge high over Bellagio. It is simply superb.

Afterwards, saturated with vastness, walkers can either retrace their steps to Guggiate or proceed to the Monte San Primo Park and catch the bus back (or take a taxi).

Fit walkers can extend this route to include the spectacular higher summit ridge of Monte San Primo – see Walk 26.

◄ From the bus stop at **Guggiate** (202m) cross the cobbled square (Piazza Sant'Andrea) and turn sharp R on Via Ciceri, flanking a villa. After a stream crossing you start up a cobbled stepped path S, winding up to houses and a road. Following signs for the 'Dorsale Lariano' (the Lariano ridge route), take the quiet surfaced road uphill through a rural area. Veering L it steepens and narrows between stone walls up to modest farms with lovely lake views (Cognanica, 304m).

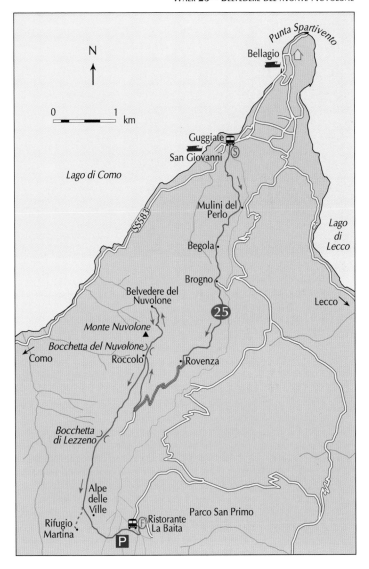

N

0 — 1 km

Punta Spartivento

Bellagio

Lago di Como

Guggiate

San Giovanni

Mulini del Perlo

Lago di Lecco

Begola

Brogno

Belvedere del Nuvolone

25

Lecco

Monte Nuvolone

Bocchetta del Nuvolone

Como

Roccolo

Rovenza

Bocchetta di Lezzeno

Alpe delle Ville

Rifugio Martina

Ristorante La Baita

Parco San Primo

P

S583

145

From the Belvedere del Nuvolone, the great Grigna stands out to the east

Still essentially S, a lane takes over, coming out at **Mulini del Perlo** (360m, 30min), where you will find old mills on a stream. An atmospheric sunken path proceeds upwards, shaded by chestnut trees on the climb to **Begola**. Here the way widens to a level lane and leads to an old property with iron railings and the scatter of houses that go under the name of **Brogno** (605m, 45min), though you'll be hard put to find a sign to that effect. The road resumes here, but you leave it soon – take care not to miss the turn R at a bridge for path n.1. Ignore the road ahead signed for Belvedere.

The narrow road S soon becomes a concrete ramp then a path through hazel woodland. A clearing with a shrine allows inspiring views south to the Monte San Primo crest. A lane now leads through the houses of **Rovenza** (723m, 30min), where there is a magnificent view of the main pyramidal Grigna peak to the east.

Still on n.1, turn R up the quiet road past farms and face 30min/200m in ascent to where a dirt lane forks R (NNE) – the relevant sign for 'Belvedere del Nuvolone' may be partly concealed by foliage. The clear way narrows to a path through woodland. Keep L at a fork in gentle ascent past several modest houses. You emerge in the clearing of the **Roccolo** (934m), an old stone hunter's hut surrounded by rowan trees hung with cages to attract birds. There are plunging views west down to the Como branch of the lake.

Nearby is the saddle **Bocchetta del Nuvolone**, where the path skirts to the R (N) around the edge of Monte Nuvolone, and heads up a brief scrambly passage. After more huts in silver birch and conifers, fork R soon for the final 5min onto the dizzy **Belvedere del Nuvolone** (1025m, 1hr). Almost at your feet is Bellagio on its lake promontory, while north is the spread of the Alps, and northeast the pyramid of Monte Legnone.

Return to **Roccolo** (934m, 30min) and either retrace your steps to **Guggiate**, allowing around 2hr 30min, or take the 'Dorsale' (crest) path into the San Primo Park, as follows.

Red/white waymarks point S through woodland with lake glimpses. At a house it widens to a lane, resuming as a level path further along. Continue through the saddle **Bocchetta di Lezzeno** (1006m) and up to a clearing with a huddle of huts and brilliant views to the Grigne, not to mention Monte San Primo, close at hand. A steady climb through beech woodland follows a barbed wire fence all the way to a meadow and pond (1182m, 1hr). Unless you still have the energy and desire for the final short 10min climb to 1221m **Rifugio Martina** – where more superb views along with delicious home-cooked meals are on offer (see Walk 26) – fork L here. An unsurfaced lane descends SE past **Alpe delle Ville** then E through beautiful beech woods. After the car park continue on to **Ristorante La Baita** and the bus stop (1100m, 30min).

WALK 26
Monte San Primo

Start/Finish	Ristorante La Baita bus stop, Parco San Primo
Distance	7.5km (4.6 miles)
Ascent/Descent	580m/580m
Difficulty	Grade 2+
Walking time	3hr 20min
Access	The ASF C36 bus links Bellagio with Parco San Primo throughout the summer months; otherwise drive to the walk start and park near Ristorante La Baita.

Thanks to the bus service, walkers can begin this must-do route to the 1682m summit of Monte San Primo at the 1100m mark, a great advantage. This memorable circuit takes you to the windswept ridge culminating in Monte San Primo, the highest point on the Triangolo Lariano. Thanks to its isolated position, towering over the Bellagio promontory, its brilliant panorama is truly something to write home about! It goes without saying that clear weather will optimise the experience.

Be aware that the route follows an extended steep and narrow path in ascent, which can get very slippery; the ridge and descent route are wider and more straightforward. Take a picnic unless you plan on eating at the popular family-run Rifugio Martina (unfortunately encountered rather too close to the start). There's always Ristorante La Baita at the end, though that means a meal without the view.

From the bus stop (1100m) near **Ristorante La Baita** in Parco San Primo, turn R on the unsurfaced lane signed for Rifugio Martina. Heading through magnificent beech woodland it swings W over a stream and past a derelict children's summer holiday home. Once through the car park and a gate, keep uphill past **Alpe delle Ville** to open pasture, then **Rifugio Martina** (1221m, 30min). This inviting eatery occupies a brilliant position with vast views up Lago di Como to the mountains beyond.

At the rear of the building a lane continues uphill to a clear signed path across meadows to follow the edge of

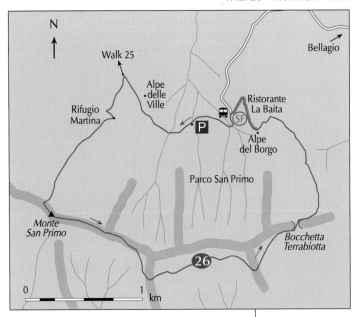

beech woods mixed with bracken. The going is already pretty steep, and loose stones and clay underfoot can make it slippery, so take your time. Pretty willow gentians and green alder shrubs brighten the way. You finally puff your way up to the crest; the summit of **Monte San Primo** and a cross (1682m, 1hr 15min) is a short climb to the L. The breathtaking views stretch towards the Po Plain and Milan, and well beyond the promontory of Bellagio up the lake to the Alps. On a fine day, you can see all the way northeast to the Matterhorn and Monte Rosa. The eastern flank of the lake features the rugged Grigne.

> The mountain's namesake, **San Primo**, was a third-century Christian martyr who was condemned to death and put in a pit with bears; but – so the story goes – the creatures turned docile and lay down at his feet. A church in his name once stood on the

Wonderful views from Rifugio Martina

mountaintop and devout Bellagians would climb up to light lamps there, but no trace remains of the building now.

The descent route takes the clear path ESE down the crest, keeping R around a knoll and crossing vast grassy slopes dotted with green alder, carline thistles and raspberries. Well below is the broad saddle of Pian del Tivano, famous for its limestone caves. Inspiring views range to the city of Lecco overshadowed by the Resegone. The broad saddle of **Bocchetta Terrabiotta** (1428m, 35min) is reached.

Cross the crest L (N) to the signpost for path n.1 (though you'll undoubtedly pause here to admire the amazing panorama down to Bellagio once more, as well as the orange roofs of Alpe del Borgo below). The path now curves towards N below Monte Ponciv, punctuated with aerials. In constant descent, you follow the edge of beautiful beech woods, and veer W to the pasture clearings of the summer farm **Alpe del Borgo** (1170m). Here a narrow surfaced road leads past defunct ski lifts and down to the road with a car park, **Ristorante La Baita** and the bus stop (1100m, 1hr) where it all began.

WALK 27

The Strada Regia from Pognana Lario to Torno

Start	Pognana Lario ferry wharf
Finish	Torno ferry wharf
Distance	10.5km (6.5 miles)
Ascent/Descent	360m/360m
Difficulty	Grade 1–2
Walking time	3hr 30min (+ 20min extra side trip)
Access	Ferries on the Como–Bellagio run stop at Pognana Lario and Torno, as do buses on the C30 line.

The ferry stop at Pognana Lario is a tiny landing stage in a quiet cove, an especially pretty spot from where to start this highly recommended route. Medieval alleys and fascinating hidden corners of laid-back lakeside villages are explored, their cosy stone dwellings linked by tunnel-like cobbled passageways. It's worth allowing extra time to explore these hamlets; there's usually someone around, looking out of a window high above, to point you in the right direction should you lose your way in the maze of streets. Mules, used for transporting goods, can still be found labouring along the way, though most have been replaced by chugging miniature mechanical carriers and tractors.

Local restaurants at Lemna and Molina can provide lunch unless you prefer a picnic.

This walk follows in the footsteps of travellers on the **Strada Regia**, the 'royal road', in use from the 1600s to the early 1900s between Como and Bellagio on the northern tip of the Lario peninsula.

▶ From the ferry wharf at **Pognana Lario** (205m) take the abrupt flight of steps that will see you puffing up to the SS583 main road and bus stop. Cross straight over for stepped Via Canzaga which leads past old houses. Turn R up Via Sant'-Antonio, then next L through a delightful linked sequence of alleys and evocative covered

Walk 28 describes another stretch of the Strada Regia, between Brunate and Torno.

151

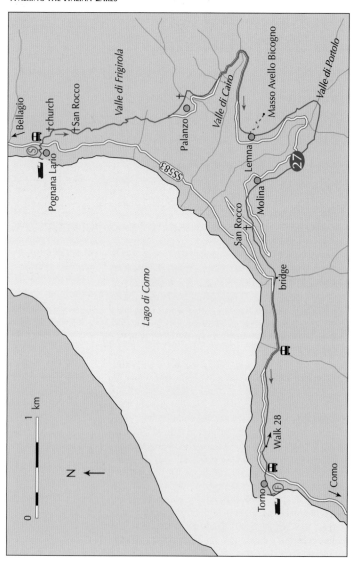

Crossing a stream on the way to Lemna

passageways. As the **church** tower comes into sight up ahead, branch R up to the building's entrance, which doubles as a superb viewing platform over the lake. Continue up past Via Crucis shrines to tarmac and a 'Strada Regia' sign. Still on Via Canzaga, keep uphill (S) past the last houses on a paved way bordered by stone walls. Past a water trough, it's not far to the **Chiesa di San Rocco** and its sweeping outlook.

A clear wide track with occasional red/white paint-splash markers proceeds S into woodland, where cascading streams are crossed on bridges in Valle di Frigirola. Gentle uphill sections lead on to the cemetery and car park at **Palanzo** (569m, 1hr). Turn L up Via Pisciola past a bar to Piazza Sant'Ambrogio and the church in grey stone. Take the old covered passageway Via Molino, which predictably (the name means 'mill'), leads across streams past an abandoned mill. Soon after keep R at a fork on a path with an iron railing, and gradually descend to join the road L, keeping an eye out for passing cars. Stick with the tarmac as it curves over the Valle di Cairo to where the Strada Regia forks off L. This takes you past another cemetery to the scenic piazza and Chiesa di San Giorgio at **Lemna** (569m, 40min).

Close at hand is a café-trattoria and an optional detour to a small tombstone from the 6th century, sculpted in an erratic boulder, as follows.

Detour to Masso Avello at Bicogno (20min return)

At the trattoria turn L uphill on the stepped way out of the houses to where the ancient tomb stands on the edge of a field, with a lovely view over the village of Molina. Return to the trattoria to resume the Strada Regia.

From the trattoria turn R, then immediately L on Via Piana. At the ensuing fork keep R under a covered passageway, then next L under an archway where the tiny traditional houses are built on bare rock. At the next junction it's L to a picturesque fountain with a green spout. Here Strada Regia signs point you R on Via Cappelletta through vegetable gardens to a chapel with a circular bench. A grassy path with an iron handrail leads in gentle descent through woodland to a stream crossing over stones in Valle di Portolo. Then it's NW up to a clearing where you can look back to Lemna and San Giorgio.

The eatery Hostaria Antica specialises in tripe, though other 'easier' dishes are served!

The route descends through the next village by way of an 1860 stone wash trough, before taking a tunnel-like passage below a building and into Piazza Sant'Antonio with the eponymous church at **Molina** (453m, 50min). ◀

Turn L on Via XX Settembre down to cross the road, following signs for Torno. After a batch of newly constructed houses, you pass through the wood to cut across the road once more, and the chapel of **San Rocco**.

Branch L here, keeping down past a concrete wall to an old way, with stone borders. Soon an elegant **bridge** leads over a ravine and around to a gap in the trees with brilliant lake views. The busy main road is soon joined L, but only for a 5min stretch due W. At a bus stop and house branch L where the lovely old path resumes high over the tarmac. Further on keep L on paved Via Vecchia per Molino past villas and well-kept gardens.

At the signed junction with the route from Piazzaga (see Walk 28) go diagonally R (Strada Regia sign) along

Lunch at Lemna

the alley Via al Pozzo, continuing under a covered passageway, then R on steps and inexorably downhill. Past a playground a path (Via Tride) leads to the main road and bus stop of **Torno** (239m, 50min). Follow the signs for 'imbarcadero' (ferry wharf, 10min) towards the divine lakeside and café.

WALK 28
Brunate to Torno Path

Start	Brunate funicular station
Finish	Torno ferry wharf
Distance	12.5km (7.7 miles)
Ascent/Descent	250m/725m
Difficulty	Grade 2
Walking time	3hr 45min (+ 1hr extra side trips)
Access	The funicular cableway station at Como is located at the far eastern end of the waterfront, close to the bus terminal and Ferrovie Nord railway station. To return to Como, catch a ferry or bus from Torno.

An immensely rewarding outing on the western side of the Lario peninsula, with a multitude of treats. The exciting funicular ride to Brunate (see Lago di Como Introduction) is immediately followed by a walk through woods home to roe deer, through delightful mountain hamlets with splendid lake views and geological highlights: intriguing glacial erratics transported from Valtellina 60km to the north by the frozen rivers, abandoned like stranded whales when the ice masses retreated. Historical interest derives from the Strada Regia, the 'royal road' (see Walk 27). The walk concludes with a well-deserved drink at the lakeside and a leisurely ferry ride back to Como. What more could anyone ask of a day out?

The route can be shortened by taking a direct descent to Torno instead of following the Piazzaga loop. Take supplies for a panoramic picnic as no restaurants or cafés are encountered.

Another beautiful section of the Strada Regia, between Pognana Lario and Torno, is described in Walk 27.

◄ On arrival at the funicular station at **Brunate** (715m) get your breath back and admire the city of Como at your feet, the moraine ridges and Monte Rosa, then take the steps in descent either side of the station to the road and viewpoint immediately over the cables. As per the Strada Regia sign, turn R past an old Campari fountain, then L down Via Nidrino with lovely Art Deco villas and Swiss-style chalets. You skirt the R edge of a playing field

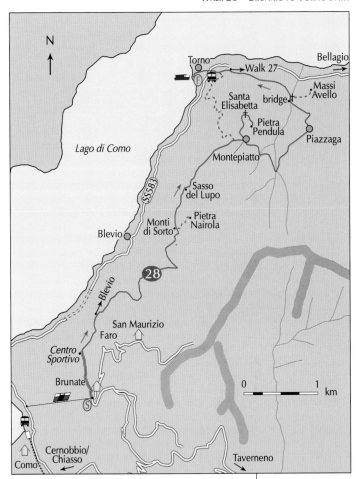

(**Centro Sportivo**) to a sign pointing you R onto a path flanking houses and N into woodland. Narrow at times and with minor ups and downs and stretches of cable handrail, the way proceeds through damp woodland with ferns and cyclamen flowers and possibly the odd fallen

At the time of writing the pathway that runs through woodland after leaving Brunate narrows occasionally where minor landslips have torn away small sections. Take a little extra care.

tree. After the fork, where a path from Blevio joins up, the path widens and improves, shifting NE but curving in and out of side valleys past minor waterfalls. ◄

At a bridge you fork L, following signs for Montepiatto, continuing on for the path junction at **Monti di Sorto** (520m, 1hr 15min), complete with a chapel, fountain and benches. There are lovely views across west to Cernobbio and the villas.

The extension to the first erratic boulder, Pietra Nairola, begins here:

Pietra Nairola side trip (40min return)
Note The steep path can be slippery. Turn R up the narrow zigzagging path to the perch of **Pietra Nairola** (620m). Appearing to totter on the slope, the 300-ton granite boulder was deposited here by a glacier which transported it from Val Masino, which branches off Valtellina at the top of Lago di Como. Return the same way to Monti di Sorto, taking extra care on the steep sections.

The clear path continues due N through the wood.

Not far along is the absolutely gigantic 4000-ton **Sasso del Lupo**, apparently in the process of sliding down the hillside. The 'wolf's rock' is so called as the hollow at its base was believed to have been the den of a dreaded wolf that ensnared disobedient children!

Soon, at a cluster of houses, keep R at a fork, in imperceptible ascent NE past huts old and abandoned. Finally join the paved mule track that ascends from the lakeside, a feasible exit route if needed, as follows.

Exit to Torno (1hr)
Turn L for the steady 400m descent down to the main road, then the lakeside and ferry wharf at **Torno** (205m).

Turn R uphill to the houses of **Montepiatto** (614m), sadly all but uninhabited apart from during holiday periods.

The Strada Regia in Torno

Make sure you fork L for the 'Chiesa' (church). In and out of the stone buildings you walk N across to the wonderful terrace of the **Chiesa di Santa Elisabetta** (45min). Shaded picnic tables welcome walkers to drink in the fantastic view across to the settlements of Moltrasio and north up this narrow stretch of Lago di Como, and to Monte San Primo (northeast), the zenith of the Triangolo Lariano.

From the church, signs point for 5min SE to another curious glacial boulder dubbed **Pietra Pendula**. A mere 60 tons, this too came from Val Masino. Granite in composition, it stands on an eroded limestone stalk, resembling a mushroom. Retrace your steps via the church (10min) and back to the main mule track through Montepiatto.

Turn L and on to the sign for Piazzaga where you go R on a paved way, leaving the houses behind. At a junction with a crucifix take the second L, a lane SE at first and mostly level. As it veers NE leave it for a path that forks off L in gentle descent through trees to a shrine in the modest settlement of **Piazzaga** (574m). Branch L (NW) down the surprisingly steep lane that becomes a long sequence of steps. These are masterfully fashioned from strips of non-slip granite sliced off an erratic boulder (necessity is the mother of invention!). Past pylons and into the wood, it curves this way and that, descending to

Montepiatto is set in dense woodland

a **bridge** (400m, 50min) over a ravine, with an adjoining chapel and signed junction for the Massi Avelli.

Massi Avelli side trip (20min return)
At the chapel fork R off the main track. A short gentle climb leads E to the abandoned hamlet of Negrenza (430m) and the first of the fascinating **Massi Avelli**, pre-Roman tombs scooped out of an erratic boulder. Several more can be found further along. Return to the bridge turn-off afterwards.

Cross the bridge and in descent WNW resume the old mule track edged with a low stone wall as it curves around the mountain and through an old gateway. Pasture, orchards and well-tended vegetable gardens line the way before the first houses of Torno are reached. At the signed junction go diagonally L (Strada Regia) along the alley Via al Pozzo, continuing under a covered passageway, then R on steps and inexorably downhill. Past a playground a path (Via Tride) leads to the main road and bus stop of **Torno** (239m, 35min). Follow the signs for 'imbarcadero' (ferry wharf, 10min) towards the divine lakeside and café.

WALK 29
Monte Boletto

Start/Finish	Brunate funicular station
Distance	10.5km (6.5 miles)
Ascent/Descent	550m/550m
Difficulty	Grade 2
Walking time	4hr 10min
Access	The departure station for the Como–Brunate funicular cableway is located at the far eastern end of the waterfront, close to the bus station and Ferrovie Nord railway station.

Rising immediately behind Bellagio, the elevated Triangolo Lariano soars to 1682m (Walk 26). Southwards it drops gradually to extensive pasture and meadows towards the plain beyond Lecco and Como. This walk uses the latter for access; long, but not particularly strenuous despite the 550m height gain, it is a bit steep at first but straightforward overall. The day begins with a thrilling 10min ride on the vertiginous funicular railway from the lakefront at Como. You disembark at Brunate, former summer resort for the wealthy, their villas set in shady woodland.

An old paved mule track leads up to the landmark Faro, a monumental though not operational lighthouse erected in 1927 to mark the centenary of the death of the inventor of the battery, Alessandro Volta, a local boy (see Walk 20). Clear paths then proceed along the ridge line touching on a host of *baitas* (rustic summer and weekend restaurants) for lunch or refreshments with wonderful views. Waymarking is patchy, but the area is well frequented and it never takes long to get your bearings.

This lovely day outing to panoramic Monte Boletto can easily be extended to take in further modest peaks by continuing on the two-day **Como–Bellagio traverse** – see www.triangololariano.it and area maps. For a shorter, Grade 1, walk limited to the wonderful Faro lookout, allow a total of 1hr 30min.

The monumental Volta lighthouse (Faro)

From the funicular station at **Brunate** (715m) follow the brown signs for 'Faro' between the cafés and souvenir stands. Past Albergo Bellavista go R after the church then L up the paved alley Via Beata Maddalena Albrici. A string of elegant villas with immaculately kept gardens can be admired during the gentle climb. The road is joined for a short stretch before the cobbled mule track resumes as Via Mulattiera, marked red/white n.1. A delightful wide and shady way, it crosses the road twice more, climbing to the roundabout at **San Maurizio** (948m, 30min), with restaurants and a hotel.

Turn L up a ramp past a lovely park a few minutes to the **Faro** lookout, a brilliant viewing point for the bottom part of the lake, the villas at Cernobbio, and the breathtaking backdrop of the Alps.

Return to San Maurizio and keep to the L of the church on Via della Regonela, aka n.1. Fork R onto a rough lane, climbing steadily due E alongside a high stone wall with tantalising glimpses of the lake through beech trees. The road and car park are reached at a restaurant and **Capanna CAO** (974m). Keep straight ahead on a mostly level track through cool conifer forest to **Baita Carla**, another rustic eatery. Now a concrete/stony track leads uphill to a junction at a house with two stone lions on guard at the entrance (sign for Pizzo Tre Termini) where you fork L (NE). A lovely path leads through copses of silver birch to a panoramic clearing.

Keep L at rusty signs up to the wooded crest and a good clear path. As the path traverses a patch of bracken take the faint route to nearby **Pizzo Tre Termini** (1144m, 1hr). The plentiful trees restrict lake views, however to the south the succession of concluding ancient moraine ridges can be admired over the plain. Continue along the

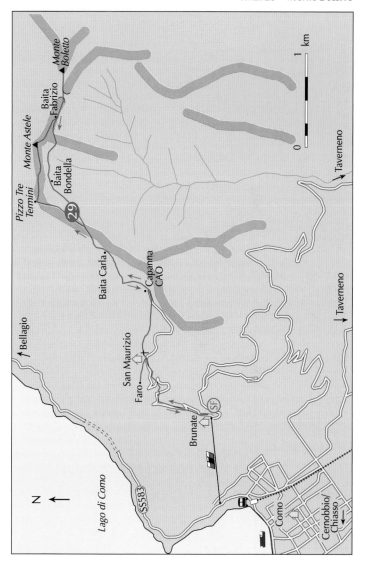

Near Pizzo Tre Termini

crest E through hazel woods via a decent lookout, then unsigned **Monte Astele** (1180m) and views to the bare ridge of Monte San Primo to the northeast. You soon drop a little, and proceed to the café-restaurant **Baita Fabrizio** (1139m, 40min).

Walk up the lane to the nearby panoramic saddle, then take the steep path R (due E) straight up the crest to **Monte Boletto** (1235m, 30min). The reward is amazing all-round views up the length of the lake, to the Grigne et al!

Afterwards return to Baita Fabrizio (1139m) and follow the concrete/stony track via the **Baita Bondella** restaurant, then past houses and through woodland. You rejoin the outward route at the house with the stone lions, above **Capanna CAO** (974m). Continue via **San Maurizio** and from there to the funicular at **Brunate** (715m, 1hr 30min).

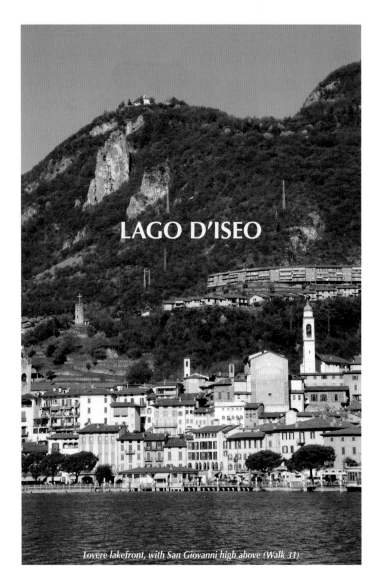

LAGO D'ISEO

Lovere lakefront, with San Giovanni high above (Walk 31)

INTRODUCTION

Little known to outsiders – and much less visited than its grander siblings – beautiful Lago d'Iseo is one of Italy's well-kept secrets. Well out of view until you actually reach its shores, it is squeezed in between the cities of Brescia and Bergamo in the region of Lombardia. Known as Sebino under ancient Roman rule, it is Italy's sixth-largest lake with a 65.3km² surface area, and boasts an attractive mountainous island, appropriately named Monteisola. Like the other lakes, Lago d'Iseo was glacially formed and is now fed by the River Oglio, which enters from the northeast through Valcamonica via a broad alluvial plain. Its northern reaches are quite dramatic and distinctly alpine in flavour as the shores are brought closer and closer together by the encroaching mountains of the Central Alps, while the south is flatter, milder and rimmed with reeds, a haven for a multitude of wildfowl. Adjoining the main town of Iseo is the territory of Franciacorta, its gentle hills planted with vineyards which produce memorable wines; not surprisingly it has been likened to a corner of Tuscany.

EXPLORING THE LAKE

The main town is **Iseo**, an especially pleasant spot in the south and a perfect base for exploring the lake. It has plenty of accommodation such as Hotel Milano (Tel. 030 980449, www.hotelmilano.info) or B&B La Terrazza (Tel. 347 6936758, www.bbiseo.it).

The township of Lovere, backed by the Alps (Walk 31)

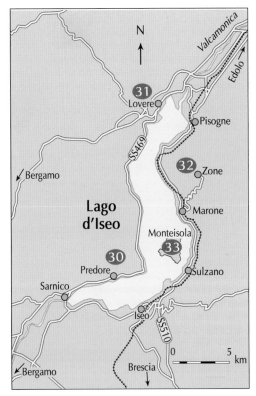

alongside a flat expanse of shallow lagoons, an important source of peat, especially during the 1930s and 1940s. Now a Nature Reserve (www.torbiere.it), it is fitted out with walkways and marked paths for birdwatchers. The lakeside is lined with campsites, such as Camping Punta D'Oro (Tel. 030 980084, www.camping-puntadoro.com).

Rising out of the centre of the lake is delightful **Monteisola**. The main port of call is Peschiera Maraglio (Tourist Office Tel. 030 9825088, www.comune.monteisola.bs.it, www.tuttomonteisola.it). All the ferries call in and there are frequent shuttles from Sulzano on the nearby eastern shore. The island even has its own bus. It is a very popular weekend destination, and the inviting lakefront restaurants do a roaring trade at lunchtime. Walk 33 climbs to the panoramic mountaintop sanctuary.

Halfway up the eastern shore of Lago d'Iseo is **Marone**, on the Le Nord railway line. It is overshadowed by the Corna Trentapassi, which is profitably

The well-organised ferry and Le Nord train services on the Brescia–Edolo line make it handy for all four walks described, and the friendly Tourist Office (Tel 030 980209, www.provincia.brescia.it/turismo) can provide timetables. There are also local bus runs by Trasporti Brescia, aka SIA. Iseo is worth a visit for its photogenic square, old streets and Romanesque churches. The settlement grew up

quarried for dolomite, processed in town; once upon a time the wool trade also brought prosperity to the area. A steep winding road climbs to Cislano. Watch out for the curious earth pyramids, the result of ongoing erosion by the mountain stream, and worth a visit. A little higher up is the alpine village of **Zone**, accessible by local bus from Marone station, with Albergo Conca Verde (Tel. 030 9870946, www.concaverde.com), and the start of spectacular Walk 32 (Tourist Office Tel. 030 9880116 www.aprotur.it).

Pisogne at the northern end of Lago d'Iseo is reachable thanks to ferries and Le Nord trains. Here a side trip is in order: a short train ride along Valcamonica sees you at Capo di Ponte and the enthralling UNESCO World Heritage Naquane National Park where vast glacially polished slabs are crammed with fascinating prehistoric graffiti, bearing witness to the artistry of early man (www.capodiponte.eu).

On the opposite shore from Pisogne and linked by ferry nestles picturesque **Lovere**, with good SAB bus services from Bergamo. Narrow alleyways and covered passages lead through an atmospheric centre punctuated with medieval towers. A worthwhile destination it also offers accommodation possibilities such as B&B Al Borgo (Tel. 34 06 301681) in the old part of town (Tourist Office Tel. 035 962178, www.comune.lovere.bg.it). It is the starting point for Walk 31 to a sanctuary on Monte Cala.

Characterising the western lakeside further south are dramatic cliffs and a number of quarries. As the lake curves west towards its conclusion, the sleepy village of **Predore** stands beneath the soaring lookout of Punta Alta, the destination for Walk 30. It can be accessed by occasional ferry or SAB buses via Sarnico from Bergamo.

Not far on is **Sarnico**, where the River Oglio exits the lake to flow southwards to join the mighty River Po.

MAPS

At a pinch the Kompass 1:50,000 walking map n.106 Lago d'Iseo Franciacorta can be used, though it is not especially up to date. Unforunately nothing else is available at the time of writing.

TRANSPORT

- Ferry timetables
  Tel. 035 971483
  www.navigazionelagoiseo.it
- Le Nord trains
  Tel. 800 500005
  www.lenord.it
- SAB buses
  Tel. 800 139392
  www.bergamotrasporti.it
- Trasporti Brescia aka SIA buses
  Tel. 840 620001
  www.trasportibrescia.it
- Zone bus
  www.comune.zone.bs.it

WALK 30
Punta Alta

Start/Finish	Predore ferry wharf
Distance	10km (6.2 miles)
Ascent/Descent	850m/850m
Difficulty	Grade 2+
Walking time	4hr 30min
Access	On the southwestern shore of Lago d'Iseo, Predore can be reached easily by bus from Bergamo or ferry from places such as Iseo.

Punta Alta is a simply magnificent lookout over the entire length and breadth of Lago d'Iseo. The walk entails a constantly steep ascent from Predore, following good clearly marked paths through beautiful woodland where clearings give lovely lake views. The only slight drawbacks are encountered during the descent: a short rough section due to erosion and fallen trees (that will hopefully be cleared), then a damnably steep surfaced farm road that can be tiring – but it does get you back to lake level pretty quickly!

Predore has grocery shops, cafés and restaurants. Take plenty of drinking water as there is none en route.

From the ferry wharf at **Predore** (187m), near a medieval tower, walk straight ahead to the main road. In Piazza Vittorio Veneto (bus stop), take the road to the L of the **Municipio**, signed for San Gregorio. Heading N up a V-shaped route excavated from the mountainside by the stream, it soon becomes unbelievably steep, narrowing past modest blocks of flats heaped on top of each other.

To ease the effort, branch L on Via Crona which leads in steps alongside a cascading stream that is soon bridged. Keep R for stepped Via Fossato to rejoin the tarmac at a **water trough** (*acquedotto*), where red/white path marking and numbering begin. For the time being puff up the surfaced road a further 5min to where n.734 forks R through a gateway. Now you embark on the flight

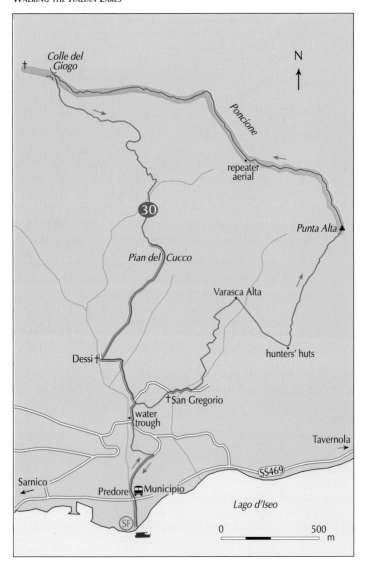

of 288 steps lined with white crosses that terminates at **San Gregorio**, aka Madonna della Neve (389m, 30min). Phew! Shaded by cypresses, the 17th-century church overlooks the village of Predore and across to Iseo and its lakes, as well as southwest to Sarnico.

Through rural landscapes of olive groves and grazing livestock, continue the uphill crusade NE on an amazingly steep concreted lane. At a fork in the lane, make sure you branch L as per n.734, which soon levels out and becomes a stony path NNE. A stream is crossed and you enter shady woodland dominated by Turkey oak, and rife with the scratching and digging evidence of wild boars. Follow red/white waymarks carefully, at many forks, to **Varasca Alta** (604m), a rocky dried-up stream and (unreliable) spring with two rock basins. A gentle climb SE between drystone walls ensues, eventually emerging from the wood at a clearing occupied by **hunters' huts** and paraphernalia (683m, 1hr). Yet more brilliant views are on offer here.

Now fork decisively L uphill NNE. The clear path ascends steadily through light woodland, where narcissus

Steep steps lead to San Gregorio

171

bloom, to gain the open and spectacular top of **Punta Alta** (953m, 45min) with its picnic bench and huge compass. Monteisola lies at your feet backed by Monte Guglielmo and Corna Trentapassi to the northeast, while north is the spread of the Orobie with the Presolana, and the snowbound Alps in the distance.

Dipping into swathes of deciduous trees, path n.707 heads essentially NW. It follows the undulating line of a wide crest through the Poncione woodland, and there are glorious glimpses on both sides down to the lake. After a repeater aerial, a gentle descent sets in, emerging from the trees at more hunters' posts. Just below is the broad and vastly panoramic grassy saddle of **Colle del Giogo** (811m, 45min).

From the saddle, just before an overgrown tower and the short climb towards the modest church, keep your eyes skinned for red/white waymarking and a faint path L (SE). The way through woodland is clear while not very well trodden, and n.735 soon appears on a signpost. A little way along it veers R (S) down a badly eroded clay

Colle del Giogo

gully. For a short stretch the going gets a bit rough and messy due to fallen trees.

The old lane soon reappears, as do rural properties and the odd house. Lined by hedgerows the way steepens and is soon surfaced. Past Pian del Cucco and meadows, it plunges to the intersection at **Dessi** (435m), a noteworthy shrine. Keep those knees braced for the near-vertical and thankfully short descent past the San Gregorio fork to the **water trough** encountered on the way up. Cut down stepped Via Fossato and return to **Predore** (187m) and the ferry wharf (1hr 30min).

A ferry arriving at Predore

WALK 31

Santuario di San Giovanni

Start/Finish	Lovere ferry wharf
Distance	6.5km (4 miles)
Ascent/Descent	450m/450m
Difficulty	Grade 1–2
Walking time	2hr 15min
Access	Lovere is served by buses from Bergamo along the western shore of the lake, and a ferry service that criss-crosses the top of Lago d'Iseo.

In the top northwestern corner of Lago d'Iseo, in the Alto Sebino district, the small town of Lovere is both hospitable and picturesque. It is understandably proud of being included on the list of 'i borghi più belli d'Italia': the most beautiful villages in Italy. Medieval towers, narrow pedestrian streets and a lively lakeside square are part of the charm. Almost directly overhead, on the prominent outcrop of Monte Cala, stands the Santuario di San Giovanni. It is easily reached by climbing from the lakeside through quiet alleyways and later woodland, with inspiring views up and down the lake en route.

From the ferry wharf and helpful Tourist Office at **Lovere** (195m) cross to the square, Piazza XIII Martiri. To the L of Pasticceria Wender take the alley Via Cavallotti to the **Polizia Municipale**. Here turn R along Via Brighenti, then L up the covered flight of steps Gradinata Ratto. At the very top, where it joins a road, fork R then take the next L on a steep street (Via Celeri) past blocks of flats, where red/white n.551 adorns a wall. Uphill a shrine is passed in memory of victims of a 1631 outbreak of the plague.

Soon afterwards is an intersection: ignore the official brown sign for Santuario San Giovanni pointing straight up the tarmac, and instead fork L on Via San Giovanni, marked red/white n.552. Quickly leaving

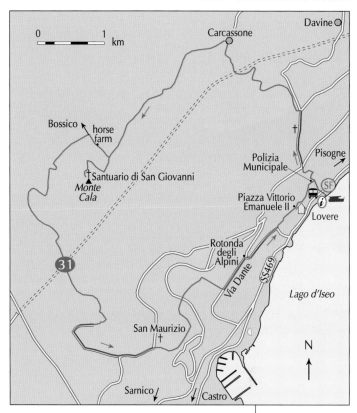

the houses behind, you climb up to join an old paved way which brings you quickly out at **Carcassone** (426m, 40min) where cool drinking water is available. Keep L on the white gravel lane W where gaps in the trees let you admire Lovere and the River Oglio flowing into the lake, the Castro promontory, and Corno Trentapassi on the opposite shore. The ascent is gentle and steady. Up at a broad saddle and turn-off, take the signed L branch for the final puff up to the church (605m, 20min).

Santuario San Giovanni was probably constructed on the site of a chapel belonging to a 12th-century fortress, of which there is no trace nowadays. Set on Monte Cala, it is a lovely shady spot for a picnic.

Return downhill and go L at the turn-off past a **horse and donkey farm** to another nearby junction by a house. Ignore the way for Bossico and go sharp L here on 'Sentiero Agrituristico Lago d'Iseo' (aka n.564) for Poltragno. A shady lane, it leads W past picnic benches, soon becoming steepish and testing knees as it heads downhill; watch out for loose stones. At a clearing it bears L past private property and onto a concreted lane. Still mostly in woodland it goes on to houses and a road, where you keep L along Via San Francesco.

Not far away at the large church/convent of **San Maurizio**, fork R off the road onto Via San Pietro, a pedestrian-only alley past the tiny chapel of the same name. The cobbled way winds down easily, keeping L at a junction, bringing you out in a residential area, where you go straight ahead to a T-junction. Branch R and continue

At Santuario San Giovanni

through a crossroads all the way down to the main road, Via Dante.

Here it's L along to the Rotonda degli Alpini with a memorial in the middle of the road. Take the lower arm of Via Oprandi to enter the old part of town on Via Matteotti, curving past medieval Torre degli Alghisi to Piazza Vittorio Emanuele II. Now Via Antonio Gramsci proceeds past another tower, Torre Soca, to the **Polizia Municipale**. Here you go R down Via Cavallotti to Piazza XIII Martiri and ferry wharf of **Lovere** (195m, 1hr 15min).

Piazza XIII Martiri at Lovere

WALK 32
Corna Trentapassi

Start/Finish	Zone cemetery
Distance	11km (6.8 miles)
Ascent/Descent	680m/680m
Difficulty	Grade 2–3
Walking time	3hr 30min
Access	From the railway station at Marone, a small bus climbs to Zone; stay on to the end, passing Piazza Almici with its solemn church, to the *cimitero* (cemetery). By car take the narrow winding road via the village of Cusato; park in the spacious car park near the cemetery.

An extremely rewarding circuit that visits Corna Trentapassi, a spectacular mountain-cum-lookout over Lago d'Iseo. To describe it as precipitous is an understatement, as it sits a head-spinning 1000m over the glittering waters. The mountain's name – '30 steps' – describes the limited extent of the summit area! This is not a walk for a windy day – or for anyone who suffers from vertigo.

Initially the walk follows part of the ancient Via Valeriana that once ran along the lake's eastern edge. Clear paths proceed through woodland to the final ascent on steep grassy slopes with loose stones. Take plenty of drinking water and food if you plan on a leisurely full-day outing. A smattering of shops and cafés are located in the lower part of Zone, but stock up beforehand if travelling by bus to avoid wasting time. The walk can be shortened marginally at the end by catching the bus from the park near San Antonio instead of returning to the cemetery.

From the **cemetery** at **Zone** (710m) walk uphill a short distance, then ignore the turn-off L for Albergo Conca Verde. Straight ahead (N) is an old cobbled lane signed as the Via Valeriana. With a gentle gradient at first, it enters conifer forest, soon reaching an interesting exposed rock slab incline that features the **fossilised footprints** of prehistoric reptiles. Not far on is a chapel, then open fields and the junction **Passo Croce di Zone** (903m, 30min).

You leave the Via Valeriana (which descends to Pisogne), and branch L (SW) on a red/white-marked path n.205. Ups and downs and a couple of narrow stretches take you through deciduous woodland, gaps in the foliage offering exciting glimpses of the lake head against a snow-capped backdrop. Bearing L inland, it passes a **saddle with a pylon**. A short climb follows to a clutch of signposts and a bench at **Forcella** (942m, 40min), where you can look back down to the villages of Cusato and Zone in their sheltered basin at the foot of Monte Guglielmo.

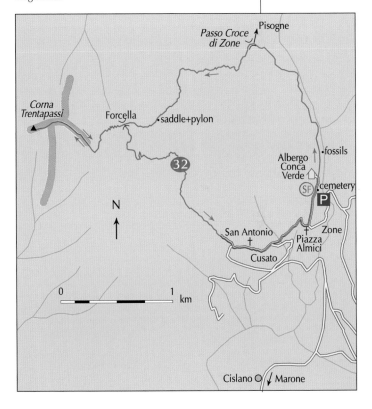

N.205 quickly ascends WSW out of the trees onto stony and grassy terrain with masses of wildflowers. It traverses diagonally L to a path junction overlooking southernmost Lago d'Iseo. Fork R (NW) now over white rock; the going gets a bit steep and scrambly in places, but with ever-improving views, and a thick carpet of flowers that burst into colour in spring thanks to the strong sunshine. Traverse a flatter section under an unnamed minor peak with a cross, then veer L (W) for the final climb to spectacular **Corna Trentapassi** (1248m, 50min). Once you've got your breath back, check out the line-up of peaks and ranges beyond the northern reaches

On Corna Trentapassi

of the lake, stretching from the Pennines, the Orobie and the Presolana in the northwest, to the Adamello.

Take the descent slowly and carefully, and watch your step on the loose stones. Return to the **Forcella** (942m, 30min), then fork R downhill on n.229. It soon becomes a broad track passing rural properties then a lovely old cobbled lane SE through woods. Houses and the road are reached at **Cusato** (689m); at a small square turn L along Via Trentapassi past the **Chiesa di San Antonio** and a park. ▶

Walk straight ahead along Via Panoramica which returns to **Piazza Almici** and a bus stop at **Zone** (680m). Fork L up the road signposted for Passo Croce di Zone to the **cemetery** (1hr).

The summit view takes in the top end of the lake with the River Oglio

To save returning to the cemetery, wait for the bus here.

WALK 33

Monteisola and the Santuario della Ceriola

Start/Finish	Peschiera Maraglio
Distance	7.5km (4.6 miles)
Ascent/Descent	420m/420m
Difficulty	Grade 1–2
Walking time	2hr 30min
Access	Year-round shuttle ferries link the island with Sulzano on the eastern shore of Lago d'Iseo; there are regular scheduled services from Iseo and other lake ports.

The attractive wooded island of Monteisola in the southeastern corner of Lago d'Iseo consists essentially of a mountain, as the name 'mountain island' suggests. A visit – and this walk – makes a lovely day outing. The locals boast that while this is nowhere near the largest lake island in Europe, at a mere 4.5km², it does hold the record for the highest elevation – 600m. The nine villages dotted around the shore are home to a thriving community of 1800 souls who earn a crust as builders of traditional fishing nets and renowned *Naèt* motor boats, not to mention as fishermen of freshwater sardines.

The island is justifiably popular as it acts as a weekend refuge from the hustle and bustle of town life; it has very few four-wheeled vehicles, and the inhabitants get around by bicycle or scooter. The orange minibus can always be taken. At Peschiera there are cafés and restaurants, as well as grocery shops.

From the ferry wharf at **Peschiera Maraglio** (205m), turn R (N) along the lakefront where fishing boats both old and new are tied up outside houses and laid-back cafés. As you reach the bakery Forneria Ziliani, branch L alongside the ochre Comune building and Tourist Office to a covered passageway. Here is the first of the signs for Santuario della Ceriola.

This way curves L at first to the start of steps through the old part of the village and up to the road. Straight across is the signed start of the path. Lined with stone

A stony path climbs towards Cure

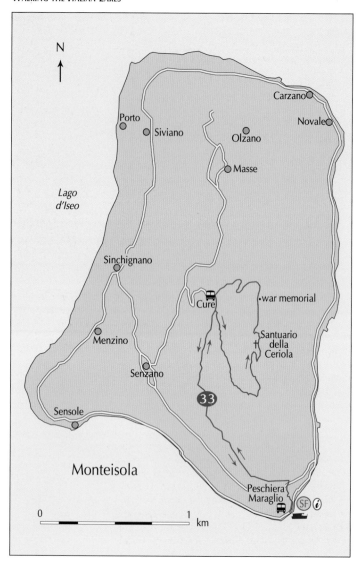

N

Carzano

Novale

Porto

Siviano

Olzano

Masse

Lago
d'Iseo

Sinchignano

Cure

•war memorial

Santuario
della
Ceriola

Menzino

Senzano

33

Sensole

Monteisola

Peschiera
Maraglio

SF ⓘ

0   1 km

Well-tended fields on the way to the sanctuary

walls, this winds and climbs W through olive groves then light woodland alive with birdsong. As it bears N the gradient levels out, enabling walkers to enjoy the glorious spread of the snow-capped Orobie range beyond the northern head of Lago d'Iseo.

Passing through cultivated fields you reach the first houses of the hillside village of **Cure** and a signed junction (466m, 1hr), where you fork R (SSE) gently uphill alongside meadows thick with wildflowers and tiny orchids. The sanctuary buildings are high above now, on the summit crest, still a fair climb away! A swing L into woodland leads across a broad flat saddle, then bears N. Not far on, just after the path resumes its climb and you're almost directly under the sanctuary building, leave the main path and fork R on an unmarked but clear path. This quickly gains the crest at a round of concrete, and goes sharp L up the easy rocky crest to the **Santuario della Ceriola** (666m, 30min). What a spot! As well as great views and the church, there's a snack bar and picnic area.

The sanctuary and much-visited **Chiesa di Madonna della Ceriola** were built on the ruins of a pagan temple. The name reputedly derives from *Quercus cerris* or Turkey oak, the wood from which its revered 12th-century statue of the Madonna was carved.

Leave the premises via the other side, through the arched portal. Go downhill and, leaving the lane as it curves left, go straight ahead down the paved stepped way lined with grey stone stations of the cross. This proceeds along a wonderfully panoramic crest, dropping to more picnic tables at a **war memorial**. Joining forces with the lane, it bears W in wide zigzags on its approach to the village of **Cure** (466m, 20min).

From here you can always return to **Peschiera** by the local bus. ◀

A seasonal bus connects Cure with Peschiera (early April–early October).

Otherwise retrace the outward route, not an unpleasant proposition as it gives you time to admire the views towards Iseo and the neighbouring marshy lakes as you return to **Peschiera Maraglio** (205m, 40min).

The old military track to Rifugio Telegrafo (Walk 46)

LAGO DI GARDA

INTRODUCTION

Shared between three regions – Lombardia, Trentino and Veneto – magnificent Lago di Garda is blessed with remarkably varied landscapes, from lakeside beaches to soaring mountains. The southern shores are very Mediterranean in flavour, lined with olive groves and vineyards, its glittering waters spreading lazily onto the plains close to the renowned city of Verona. However the most impressive part is the breathtaking northern sweep where the lake is squeezed between dramatic cliffs hundreds of metres high, creating stiff breezes which race across the surface of the water, much to the delight of keen yachtsmen and windsurfers. Towering above it all is the splendid Monte Baldo massif, a haven for walkers and paragliders.

Garda is the largest lake in Italy with a total surface area of 370km², 125km in circumference, 51km in length and 17km across at its widest point. Its old Roman name was 'Benacus' after the god who protected the lake and its inhabitants: a comforting thought.

Its beauty has been appreciated since ancient times when the poet Catullus described it as a 'pearl' – and generations of illustrious writers, artists and musicians have found inspiration and romance here. DH Lawrence eloped to Lake Garda in 1912 with his beloved Frieda. He may have heard about it through the writings of the great German philosopher Johann Wolfgang von Goethe who sang its praises (1786), noting: 'How I wish my friends were here for a moment to enjoy the view I have before me!' They certainly heeded his words, as Lago di Garda has been a summer playground for northern Europeans for centuries. Poor Byron was not so lucky or optimistic and commented grumpily in 1816: 'Terrible weather. Poured with rain. It would have been better not to have come.'

EXPLORING THE LAKE

The southern end of Lago di Garda has two resorts with a distinctly seaside feel: Peschiera and Desenzano (Tourist Office Tel. 030 3748726, www.provincia.brescia.it/turismo), both on the Milan–Verona–Venice railway line. They are good entry points for the lake and have regular ferry services, but lie rather too far south to be useful as a base for walkers. Halfway between the two is the Sirmione peninsula, a spectacular finger of land that terminates with a picturesque castle and a vast ancient Roman resort, the Grotte di Catullo: well worth a visit.

Running up the western edge of the lake is the SS572/SS45b, with

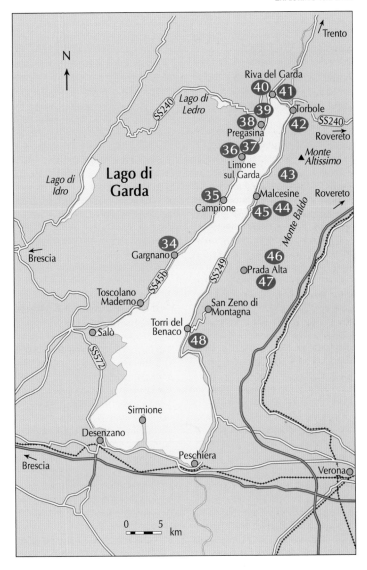

N

Trento

Lago di
Ledro

SS240

Riva del Garda
40 41

39 Torbole
38 42
Pregasina SS240
Rovereto

36 37
Limone Monte
sul Garda Altissimo

Lago di
Idro

43

Lago di
Garda

35 Malcesine Rovereto
Campione 45 44

Monte Baldo

34
Brescia 46
Gargnano
Prada Alta
SS249 47

Toscolano
Maderno
San Zeno di
Montagna

Salò
Torri del
Benaco
48
SS572

Sirmione

Desenzano

Brescia
Peschiera

Verona

0   5
km

plentiful bus services by Trasporti Brescia (also known as SIA) all the way north to Riva del Garda. **Salò**, 22km up, is the first town of interest, a procession of magnificent villas and grand hotels from the late 1700s and 1800s. Many were occupied by Mussolini and his cohorts in 1943 in a last-ditch attempt to keep fascism alive under the short-lived RSI (Repubblica Sociale Italiana), which struggled on until Italy was liberated by the partisan forces and the Allies in 1945. (A local association organises themed excursions along the western shoreline: visit www.asar-garda.org.)

A further 6km on is **Toscolano Maderno**, where the mid-lake car ferry from Torri del Benaco docks. Its bulging delta, created, over time by the River Toscolano, is a haven for campers. The watercourse was also the reason for the development of paper mills in Valle delle Cartiere, now industrial archaeological sites. Of the plentiful hotels there's centrally located Albergo Giardino (Tel. 0365 641360, www.albergo-giardino.com) in the traffic-free part of town (Tourist Office Tel. 030 3748741, www.provincia.brescia.it/turismo).

Another 8km north, accessible by Brescia Trasporti bus or ferry, is photogenic **Gargnano** that so charmed DH Lawrence with its lemon gardens. They would be covered over with scaffolding and roofed with planks in the cold winter months to protect the precious fruit, and fires lit inside to ward off freezing conditions. The economic

peak for the cultivation of lemons was in the mid-1800s; thereafter a disease decimated the crops, while the *coup de grâce* was the discovery of a synthetic form of citric acid, combined with competition from groves on the Amalfi Coast, from which the local industry never recovered. Stay at delightful lakeside Hotel Bartabel (Tel. 0365 71330, www.hotelbartabel.it) or Hotel Garni Riviera (Tel. 0365 72292 www.garniriviera.it). The Tourist Office is on the main road opposite the bus stop (Tel. 0365 791243, www.gargnanosulgarda.it). Walk 34 sets out from here, climbing to the beautiful cliffside Eremo di San Valentino.

The ensuing narrower stretch of the SS45b is responsible for the road's notoriety as it comprises sequences of tunnels bored through lakeside cliffs where drivers have to deal with rapidly alternating sunlight and shade. It was not put through until 1931 as the extremely steep cliffs made road construction challenging to say the least. Film buffs will recognise the road in a car chase from the 2008 James Bond film *Quantum of Solace*.

An abrupt turn-off 11km from Gargnano leads to tiny **Campione** squeezed up against a sheer cliff on a small fan of fluvial detritus. An important industrial centre as early as medieval times, with mills and metalworking enterprises powered by harnessing the impetuous Torrente di San Michele that flows through a dramatic rocky chasm, it had paper and cotton mills in the 1900s when a model

Malcesine's inviting lakefront

village was constructed for the workers. Campione is currently undergoing a transformation as a smart sailing resort. The lakeside bus service calls in here and Walk 35 explores the exciting chasm as well as climbing to the hilltop villages. The cafés and grocery shop are useful for walkers.

Next en route is delightful **Limone sul Garda**, likewise constructed right up against the cliffs in a wonderful position overlooking a bay yet protected from prevailing winds and sun drenched year-round. It is crowded with dozens of flourishing terraces which once supported citrus and lemon plantations, as the name would suggest (although scholars insist it derives from either *limen* for 'border' or *lima* for 'river'). JW Goethe wrote this inviting description after a trip by rowing boat: 'We went past

Limone, whose mountainside gardens, arranged in terraces and planted with lemon trees, have a rich and well-kept appearance. The whole garden consists of rows of square white pillars, placed at certain intervals, which ascend the mountain in steps.'

Frequent ferries on the Malcesine–Riva del Garda circuit – and many on the complete lake run – call in at the pretty port alongside colourful fishing craft. Lakefront accommodation includes Hotel Azzurro (Tel. 0365 954000, www.hotelh.com) and Hotel Sole (Tel. 0365 954055 www.hotel-solelimone.com). There's a Tourist Office on the main road near the bus stop and another on the lakefront (Tel 0365 918987 or 0365 954265, www.visitlimonesulgarda.com). Stay here for Walk 36, a wonderful exploration of the wild Val del Singol, and Walk

37, the leisurely 'Sentiero del Sole' (sun path) that wanders along the lakefront.

The peaceful village of **Pregasina**, accessible from Riva del Garda via a long road tunnel near Lago di Ledro, is visited on Walks 38 and 39 and has aptly named Hotel Panorama (Tel. 0464 559045, www.hotelpanorama-apregasina.com).

At the very top of the lake is the lively market town of **Riva del Garda** with a picturesque traffic-free heart of old streets crammed with shops and houses, overseen by battlements. In the main lakeside square is Hotel Centrale (Tel. 0464 552344, www.hotelcentralegarda.it).

Riva has a large bus terminal at the rear of the old town: Trentino Trasporti is responsible for services to Rovereto railway station as well as the rare service to Pregasina; ATV runs down the eastern side of the lake and on to Verona, while Trasporti Brescia/SIA covers the western shore. The centrally located Tourist Office is contactable at Tel. 0464 554444, www.gardatrentino.it. Walks 39, 40 and 41 begin in Riva, and Walk 38 takes a bus from here.

Torbole occupies the top north-eastern corner of the lake, and lies in the shadow of Monte Altissimo, the northernmost outlier of mammoth Monte Baldo. It has plenty of buses on the Riva–Rovereto and Riva–Verona lines, as well as ferries on the Malcesine–Limone circuit. Walk 42 begins here, close to the Tourist

Gargnano (Walk 34)

Limone and its lemon groves squeezed below soaring cliffs

A VENETIAN VICTORY

Back in the year 1438 the mighty Venetian Republic was threatened on its western border by the powerful Visconti of the Duchy of Milan, who were extending their control across the Po Plain. In no position to engage in full-scale warfare, Venice devised an ingenious plan: they would surprise the enemy's armada on Lago di Garda by approaching stealthily from the north. The strategic importance of this undertaking is reflected in its astronomical cost – a hefty 15,000 ducats.

A fleet of 33 longboats and galleys set sail from the lagoon to navigate the Adige River to Verona then north via a series of locks, a voyage of 200km. South of Rovereto the craft began the hard part: 25km overland to Torbole dragged by 2000 paired oxen, using tree trunks as rollers for the laborious climb. Hundreds of labourers cleared mountainsides and erected bridges; robust cables and winches ensured a safe passage for the steep descent to the lakeside. Unfortunately the earth-moving operations had not gone unnoticed and the Milanese awaited the Venetians at Desenzano harbour; defeat was inevitable, and only two galleys escaped capture. However, all was not lost. Two years later a new fleet was assembled and victory resounding, thus bringing the entire lake under Venetian control.

Office (Tel. 0464 505177, www. gardatrentino.it). This unassuming lakeside village was the setting for a fascinating tale starring a 15th-century Fitzcarraldo of the Venetian Republic (see above).

Dominated by the colossal bulk of Monte Baldo, the SS249 heads south from Torbole for 14km to the picturesque town of **Malcesine**, its medieval heart still intact. Perched on a rocky promontory, it grew up around a castle erected by the lords of Verona, the Scaligeri. Enjoy the views from the battlements and tower, and render homage to JW Goethe, who risked arrest here in 1786 when his innocent sketching generated suspicions that he was spying for the Hapsburgs! It was during a sojourn at Malcesine in the summer of 1913 that the young Austrian artist Gustav Klimt hired a rowing boat to paint the town from the water in inspiring pastel hues.

The huge range of accommodation includes central Hotel Alpino (Tel. 045 7400053, www.hotelalpinomalcesine.it). Frequent ferries and ATV buses on the Verona–Riva del Garda run call in. From May to October a Tourist Bus shuttles back and forth between Malcesine and Cassone (4km away), where you can stay at Hotel Cassone (Tel. 045 6584197, www.hotelcassone.com). The helpful main Tourist Office is close to the harbour at Malcesine and a smaller information point operates near the bus stop (Tel. 045 7400044, www.tourism.verona.it, www.malcesinepiu.it).

Monte Baldo, rising high above the town, boasts awesome views. This forbidding limestone barrier runs north–south for 40km, separating Lago di Garda from the Adige valley-cum-traffic artery. It consists of a string of tops: Altissimo, Cima delle Pozzette, Telegrafo and the highest, Valdritta, at 2218m. The massif remained high and dry during the ice ages, a refuge for unique species of alpine flora and earning it the title 'Botanical Garden of Europe'. It can easily be reached thanks to an ultra-modern two-stage cable car from Malcesine, complete with revolving cabins, that glides over the olive groves and up to dizzy Bocca Tratto Spino for Walks 43 or 44.

Whereas Walk 45 begins from the intermediate cable-car station at San Michele where Locanda Monte Baldo offers rooms with a view (Tel 045 7401679, www.locandamontebaldo.com), it is also possible to drive this far up from the lakeside. The lovely southernmost section of Monte Baldo, the best area for wildflower seekers, is accessed from Prada Alta – see below. (**Note** It's best to wait until mid-June to embark on walking routes on Monte Baldo to ensure they are snow-free – check locally.)

About halfway down the eastern shore of Lago di Garda is peaceful **Torri del Benaco** with a pretty harbour and pedestrian-only centre dominated by a medieval castle-museum whose battlements double as a wonderful lake belvedere. It also boasts one of the few working *limonaie* (lemon groves) on Lago di Garda (Tourist Office Tel. 045 7225120, www.tourism.verona.it). Torri is well served by ATV buses and frequent car ferries across to Toscolano Maderno, though few passenger services around the lake. Set at the port is lovely Hotel Gardesana (Tel. 045 7225411, www.gardesana.eu), while less expensive and a short stroll away is Onda Garni (Tel. 045 7225895, www.garnionda.com). Walk 48 departs from Torri to explore a clutch of modest rock engravings.

High above at 580m, **San Zeno di Montagna**'s cool air is a great attraction for midsummer holidaymakers. It is linked to Torri del Benaco and Verona by decent ATV bus runs. The village is strung out along a panoramic ridge, and in summer the air is thick with the divine scent of lime trees. It has a scattering of shops, and a Tourist Office (Tel 045 6289296, www.comunesanzenodimontagna.it); friendly Hotel Centrale Tel. 045 7285111 www.bbalbergocentrale.it); Hotel Bellavista (Tel. 045 7285286, www.bellavistahotel.eu); and Taxi (Tel. 045 7285590, Mob. 337 471658).

The road continues 6km northeast to **Prada Alta** set at 1000m, with the chair lifts up the eastern flanks of Monte Baldo explored in Walks 46 and 47. There's accommodation at hotel/campsite Edelweiss (Tel. 045 6289039, www.edelweiss-hotel.it), which also runs a well-stocked supermarket. A handy summer Walk&Bike

Goethe is remembered at Malcesine

bus organised by ATV from Verona draws in here on an almost daily basis. (**Note** It stops at the car park near the main Chiesa di San Zeno di Montagna, before continuing up to Prada Alta.)

MAPS

Kompass sheet n.102 Lago di Garda, 1:50,000 covers all the walks with varying levels of accuracy. For greater detail, Riva del Garda Tourist Information sells a good 1:30,000 map for Walks 36–42, and Lagiralpina do two excellent 1:25,000 maps – n.12 'Alto Garda' covers Walks 35–45 and n.20 'Monte Baldo' is good for Walks 35, 44–48. (Lagiralpina maps are sold widely at Lago di Garda; they can also be ordered by email from the

Limonaia at Torri del Benaco

publisher at lagiralpina@gmail.com or through www.cartoguide.it – click on 'negozio' shop). Kompass map n.694 1:25,000 'Parco Alto Garda Bresciano' covers Walk 34.

TRANSPORT

- ATV buses
  Tel. 045 8057922
  www.atv.verona.it
- Ferry timetables
  Tel. 800 551801
  www.navlaghi.it
- Malcesine cable car
  www.funiviedelbaldo.it
- Prada Alta lifts
  www.funiviedelgarda.it
- Trasporti Brescia Nord/SIA buses
  Tel. 840 620001
  www.trasportibrescia.it
- Trentino Trasporti buses
  Tel. 0461 821000
  www.ttesercizio.it

WALK 34

Eremo di San Valentino

Start/Finish	Gargnano bus stop
Distance	10km (6.2 miles)
Ascent/Descent	650m/650m
Difficulty	Grade 2
Walking time	3hr 45min
Access	Gargnano has plenty of buses from Toscolano Maderno; slightly fewer from Riva di Garda and Limone. Ferries also call in. By car you can drive as far as Sasso, cutting the walk time to 1hr 15min.

The Eremo di San Valentino is a magical spot: a tiny church and hermit's dwelling sheltering under a dramatic cliff hanging off a rugged mountain. The modest building is invisible to the naked eye from the lakeside as it blends perfectly into its rocky surroundings. It overlooks Gargnano, a particularly pretty town halfway along the western shore of Lago di Garda and a lovely spot to spend a couple of nights.

Passing the old gardens and orchards at the foot of sheer cliffs, the walk climbs 650m on cobbled lanes and paths through woodland with a distinctly Mediterranean flavour. En route are local shrines known as *santelle*, as well as frequent red/white CAI waymarking. The walk touches on the village of Sasso, an alternative entry point (via rare bus from Gargnano) where the justifiably popular way branches off for the Eremo.

LEMON GROVES

The district is dotted with elegant villas designed for the bourgeoisie of the late 18th to 19th century, alongside flourishing olive groves and splendid traditional *limonaia* plantations. DH Lawrence wrote 'rows of naked pillars rising out of the green foliage like ruins of temples: white square pillars of masonry, standing forlorn in their colonnades and squares, rising up from the mountain-sides here and there, as if they remained from some great race that had once worshipped here'. Many of these old agricultural properties have been converted into residences with wonderful gardens.

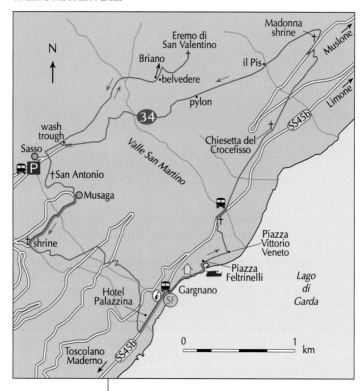

From the bus stop on the main road opposite the Tourist Office at **Gargnano** (66m), follow the sign for 'passaggio pedonale' down steps by a car park. This quickly brings you onto the walkway that leads L (NE) along the lake's edge, a lovely start to this route. At the charming port and ferry wharf go L across **Piazza Feltrinelli** to pick up Via Roma R. Beneath elegant palaces, continue to **Piazza Vittorio Veneto** and branch L up Via Parocchia. Steps lead up to a water distributor alongside a huge pink colonnaded church, set on the main road. To the R a matter of metres on the opposite side of the road is a bus stop and map board (15min), and the start of Via Crocefisso, waymarked red/white for CAI n.30. Soaring almost over-head is the pale mountain outcrop where the Eremo nes-tles, before rising to Monte Comer.

Moving off NNE the cobbled lane makes a gentle, steady ascent screened by stone walls retaining the mar-vellous terraced gardens of lemons, olives and grapes which spill out over the way, accompanied by straggling bouquets of caper plants. Interesting information boards are set along the route. The tiny yellow **Chiesetta del Crocefisso** is passed, and you soon cross the road for Muslone. As the way steepens, there are plenty of oppor-tunities for drinking in views east across the lake to the heights of Monte Baldo. A curve L sees you heading up through wood to the road once more.

Fork R along the asphalt for a matter of metres to where a lane resumes past a showy majolica **Madonna shrine**. Not far up you fork L (SW) on n.30 for a steep stretch that leads through woods to an overhang and dry white torrent bed, **il Pis** (303m). Here the lane ends at a house, and a path takes over for steeper rocky walking W. At a power line and **pylon**, and an excellent lookout, a variant route turns sharp R – experts only as it entails an exposed scramble – but you proceed L under bright red cliffs. The way soon follows old stone terracing, then joins a lane near a house and Valle San Martino. It's not far up to a group of new houses, where you branch R on tarmac.

Only minutes uphill is the laid-back village of Sasso (520m, 1hr) looking over to twin peaks Monte Castello and Pizzocolo. However, before you reach the village centre fork R on Via Sasso (aka n.31), and R again at the **wash trough**. An old paved way leaves the settlement NE, climb-ing easily through shady woodland to a superb **belvedere** with bird's-eye views to Gargnano, Monte Baldo opposite, and down the sweep of the lake to the Sirmione peninsula. Ignore the fork L for Briano, and keep R, soon to plunge down a gully on good steps. The path then leads L around to a door – push it open and up the staircase to the divine hideout of the **Eremo di San Valentino** (712m, 40min). Cypress trees shield the tiny church and rooms built onto the overhanging rock face. A true place for meditation.

The walk follows the lakeside at Gargnano

In 1630 the plague struck and claimed 400 victims. The remaining population fled to the mountainous hinterland for refuge; once the 'all clear' sounded and people could return to their lakeside homes, survivors built the church of the **Eremo di San Valentino** in gratitude. In 1842 it reportedly became the hideout for a local man avoiding military call-up.

Afterwards – duly refreshed – retrace your steps, but at the **wash trough** keep straight on to the square of **Sasso** (520m, 35min), with a café. If you don't time your arrival for one of the rare buses that link with Gargnano, then fork L at the handy map board and soon R, flanking a playing field (n.19). This lane soon curves L below the **Chiesa di San Antonio** with breathtaking views across the glittering lake that will take your mind off the near-vertical descent towards the rooftops of **Musaga** (454m). Red/white markings lead down through alleys in the well-kept village.

After veering R down through a covered passageway, a short stretch L (SW) leads along a little-used road. At a prominent **shrine** branch L (E) on n.37, the concrete lane Via al Pastore. This leads in rapid descent past farms and across the road for a steep stony path. After a further road crossing it becomes Via dei Mulini, once home to numerous water-powered mills. Steps lead past a sequence of houses to a concrete lane. The gradient finally eases a little as you veer R across a stream and cut over the road once more. A narrow path takes over, flanked by stone walls. This brings you out on tarmac near **Hotel Palazzina** and shortly at the main lakeside road, where you go L for the short distance back to the bus stop at **Gargnano** (66m, 1hr).

The rock overhang at Eremo di San Valentino

WALK 35

Campione to Pregasio Loop

Start/Finish	Campione, Piazza Arrighini
Distance	9.7km (6 miles)
Ascent/Descent	670m/670m
Difficulty	Grade 2
Walking time	4hr
Access	A short detour off the SS45b as it passes through tunnels between Gargnano and Limone, Campione is served by Trasporti Brescia buses, as is Pregasio (an alternative entry or exit point). No ferries call in at Campione.

Campione is an amazing spot, a cluster of historic factories set on a tiny alluvial fan 'island' beneath sheer cliffs that soar a good 500m skywards. This industrial archaeology now takes second place to a brand-new residential development for sailing and windsurfing enthusiasts. It currently offers a couple of cafés and restaurants, along with a modest supermarket.

This is an exhilarating circuit that climbs high above the dramatic cliffs. Both start and finish sections follow long flights of steps dug out of the cliff face to penetrate the dramatic ravine where the Torrente San Michele has spent centuries wearing away the limestone and sculpting a deep narrow course. Its waters have been exploited since medieval times as a source of power for industry at Campione. The path goes through a 200m-long tunnel, with minimal electric lighting; take a torch or headlamp. The middle section wanders through peaceful farmland hundreds of metres above the lake, touching on villages such as Pregasio.

From centrally located Piazza Arrighini at **Campione** (67m), head in the direction of the lake and take the footbridge R across Torrente San Michele, and R (SW) again up steps marked as n.267. This leads over the road for the start of the fascinating old route that climbs steeply, aided by a handrail. It passes beneath water conduits on arched supports as the ravine of the Torrente San Michele plunges far below. The path goes through a low

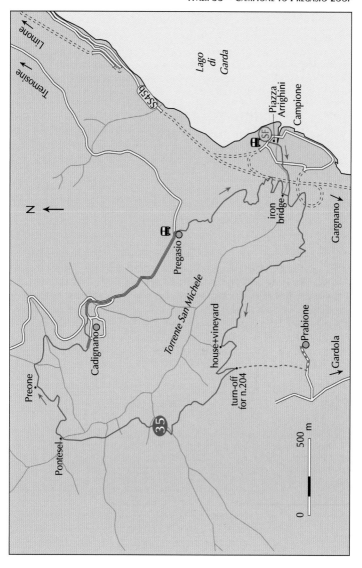

203

rock tunnel with some lighting – watch your head! – and emerges into daylight again to follow man-made canals and pools.

Ignore the R fork across the **iron bridge** (30min, the return route) and keep L on n.266. Initially SW this quickly becomes a superbly spectacular path close to the cliff edge with brilliant views over Lago di Garda from Monte Baldo and Malcesine to Campione at your feet. Bearing R (W) it levels out, entering woodland thick with smoke bush and hornbeam. A little way in, take care not to miss the **turn-off R for n.204** signed for Pontesel.

> A short detour off the outward route from the turn-off is the village of **Prabione** and the Visitor Centre of the Parco Alto Garda Bresciano (Tel. 0365 761642 www.parcoaltogarda.eu).

It's a gentle descent through chestnut woodland with lovely views back to the ravine and the lake beyond. At a modest vineyard and small house, fork L up a lane for a short winding climb to join a broader lane, still n.204

Rural landscape on the way to Pontesel

Campione at the foot of cliffs

(500m). This proceeds N in gradual descent past another modest house and narrows to a path that drops decisively through woodland to the amazing cleft gorge crossed by the tiniest stone bridge that is **Pontesel**, aka Ponticello (290m, 1hr 30min).

The clear path continues through dense jungle-like vegetation with masses of ferns, occasionally along natural limestone ledges, finally reaching a rural landscape and cultivated fields. Follow red/white waymarks up to a Y-junction (**Preone**) where you fork R on n.203. The level

The chasm at Pontesel

lane heads essentially SE to flank olive plantations before joining the tarmac at **Cadignano**.

It's not far downhill to the village of **Pregasio** (477m, 50min), with cafés and a bus service. At the start of the buildings, turn R immediately opposite the supermarket down Via Lomas – ignore the archway and fork R at house n.10 down steps and past a gate, then L at the corner of the garden. A path leads down to a lane, n.267 heading S in a rural landscape of olive groves and orchards. At the many forks take care to follow the red/white markings onto a path through oak woods and soon a long stretch hewn into the rock face. This descends into the ravine on a thrilling cliffside path, climbs over a central outcrop and finally reaches the **iron bridge** (50min) encountered on the way up.

From here, return to the lakeside and **Campione** (67m, 20min) by reversing your outward route.

WALK 36

Limone sul Garda and the Valle del Singol

Start/Finish	Limone sul Garda, Lakeside Tourist Office
Distance	10km (6.2 miles)
Ascent/Descent	880m/880m
Difficulty	Grade 3
Walking time	4hr 30min
Access	Limone sul Garda can be reached by ferry as well as and buses from Riva del Garda (Trentino Trasporti) and Gargnano and southern towns (Trasporti Brescia).

A wonderfully rewarding circuit for walkers with good stamina and path-tested knees, climbing high into beautiful and craggy Val del Singol. Enjoy a picnic on the higher central section before an exhilarating plunge down steep and rocky Val Pura. The walk starts and concludes in the attractive lakeside village of Limone sul Garda, beset with *limonaie*, abandoned lemon terraces now reminiscent of ancient temples.

It rates Grade 3 for several narrow central sections that are both steep and exposed at times, and walking boots with a good grip are recommended. This route should be avoided in bad weather as it may be dangerous. That said, a simple stroll up the lane in Valle del Singol is worthwhile in all weathers.

At **Limone sul Garda** (66m) from the lakeside Tourist Office turn uphill on the steps of Via Rovina, then follow the narrow paved road that proceeds up to the main road Via IV Novembre. ▸

Straight over is pedestrian-only Via Milanesa, with red/white marking for path n.101. The cobbled way proceeds through the residential area and between old lemon terraces, their walls dripping with caper vines.

Go under an old arch to **Bar La Milanesa** and soon cross a bridge over Torrente San Giovanni. No traffic is allowed beyond this point in beautiful Valle del Singol: its apt name means 'narrow, drawing in'. Heading NW

A short distance left is the main bus stop close to Bar Turista and a second Tourist Office.

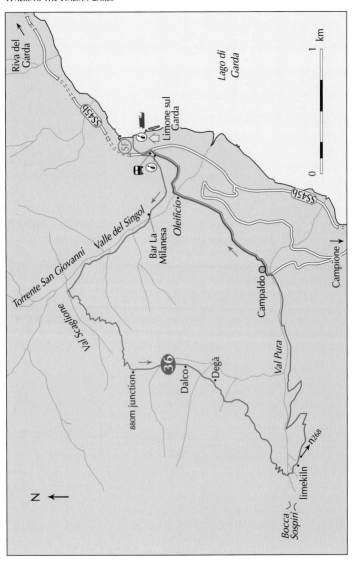

after a waterfall and a limekiln, ignore the n.111 fork L for Dalco and stick to the lane, soon to a drinking-water point (Acqua del Singol). The stream cascades alongside the lane, while well beyond, inland, are soaring crags: Préals, Corno Vecchia and Traversole.

Clear views of Limone during the ascent of Val Scaglione

Fork L (460m, 45min) on path n.102 up Val Scaglione through conifer woodland and heather. You climb SW above a dry stony streambed to a shoulder, the terrain more and more dramatic with every step. The lakeside township of Limone is seen clearly below on its alluvial fan created by the mountain stream flowing down Valle del Singol.

About halfway up is a short exposed ledge, then the zigzagging resumes and you finally emerge at a welcome clearing and **path junction** (880m, 1hr 15min). Bear L (S) on n.110 to a house and the ruined church at **Dalco** (842m). A gentle uphill stretch SW follows the clear old path to two houses in a lovely setting amid beech and huge conifers. The sunken path now continues to the signed junction of **Degà** (904m, 30min), where you need n.268 for Limone.

With a brilliant lake panorama you soon find yourself plunging SW on a clear if narrow and madly zigzagging path across scree gullies beneath Bocca Sospiri. A wider track is gained at a memorial plaque and **limekiln**, and you soon need to leave n.268 to fork L (E) on n.123, a narrow steep path down wild Val Pura, reminiscent of the wilder scenery of the Dolomites. The curves help take some of the sting out of the abrupt descent. The torrent is crossed further down and a concreted lane joined to lead to the houses of **Campaldo** (220m, 1hr 15min).

Here turn L along a surfaced road in steady descent NE. At an intersection keep L past the former lemon orchard, now labelled 'Casa natale' (birthplace) San Daniele Comboni, a local missionary. Take the lower road here downhill past an **oleificio** (olive press) and a grocery shop at a three-way junction – keep L across Torrente San Giovanni close to the opening of Valle del Singol. Over a rise and down Via Caldogno and you're back at the Tourist Office on the main road near the bus stop at Bar Turista. It's not far back to the lakeside Tourist Office at **Limone sul Garda** (66m, 45min), the perfect place for a well-deserved refreshing drink.

WALK 37
Sentiero del Sole

Start/Finish	Limone sul Garda ferry wharf
Distance	6.5km (4 miles)
Ascent/Descent	180m/180m
Difficulty	Grade 1 as far as Hotel Panorama, then Grade 2
Walking time	3hr
Access	Limone sul Garda can be reached by ferry as well as buses from Riva del Garda (Trentino Trasporti) and Gargnano and southern towns (Trasporti Brescia).

Initially the Sentiero del Sole 'sun path' follows a delightful old lane parallel to the beautiful lake, passing hotels, olive terraces and several typical *limonaie*, lemon orchards. After crossing the main road the latter section traverses loose rocky terrain that earns it a Grade 2, but it is not especially difficult. It makes its way up mountain flanks to a beautiful belvedere point, formerly a wartime position. The Sentiero del Sole takes a lower return path to Hotel Panorama before retracing its steps to Limone.

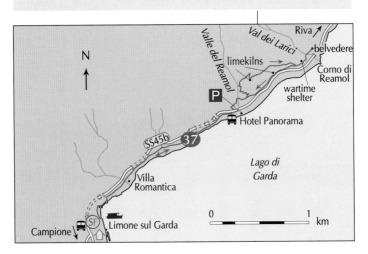

En route it is feasible to detour to a albeit modest beach for a well-deserved swim, as per the sign near Villa Romantica Hotel.

◀ From the ferry wharf at **Limone sul Garda** (66m) take Via Nova lined with rock walls as it curves R, heading NE past Chiesa San Rocco and through an arched passageway. Hotels are dotted along the way; ahead rise the sheer cliffs of Punta Larici. High above a shingle beach you cross the Rio Sé in an area of olive groves with views over to Monte Baldo and the Altissimo mountain. At **Villa Romantica** Hotel and an adjacent *limonaia* ignore the lane for the *spiaggia* (beach) and keep L up the surfaced lane. At a signed fork and drinking tap, go R for Sentiero del Sole, Via Reamol.

A cobbled way, it touches on pretty villas and charming gardens punctuated with cactus, and is a leisurely promenade on the lake edge between Mediterranean plants and soaring cliffs. Further along a gentle slope leads up to the main road where you turn R along a walkway. Soon cross to the other side and the car park for **Hotel Panorama** (115m, 40min); a bus stop is close at hand.

The path hugs the lakeside

Here turn L up the gravel path past cypress trees and pines to pass huge nets that retain rockfalls. The path

leads across a dry streambed in Valle del Reamol directly above the hotel buildings. As you wind uphill, steeply at times, follow the signed forks carefully. Benches occupy strategic positions for appreciating lake views. After tight zigzags is an excellent lookout and path junction (240m) where you ignore n.122 for Punta Larici, and instead go R in descent. This touches on an old limekiln (*calchera*) in light woodland bright with cyclamens and Mediterranean flora such as rockroses.

The scenic path continues E to a water tank above the lemon orchards of Reamol, then heads downhill on loose stones. It curves around rockslide barriers then bears L on a level past a **wartime shelter** and trenches dating back to World War II. Soon Val dei Larici is traversed and the broad curves of an old military track lined with stone walls lead up to a rocky point and **belvedere** with seats and a World War I position above **Corno del Reamol** (1hr). Marvellous views across the head of Lago di Garda to Torbole and Monte Baldo can be enjoyed.

Return to the barriers but keep L this time, and Sentiero del Sole waymarks reappear. Parallel to the road it passes along olive terraces and by another abandoned limekiln. Further along the path climbs R to rejoin the outward route; turn L to cross the dry torrent bed directly above Hotel Panorama, and re-descend to the car park for **Hotel Panorama** (115m, 40min).

Retrace your steps to **Limone sul Garda** (66m, 40min).

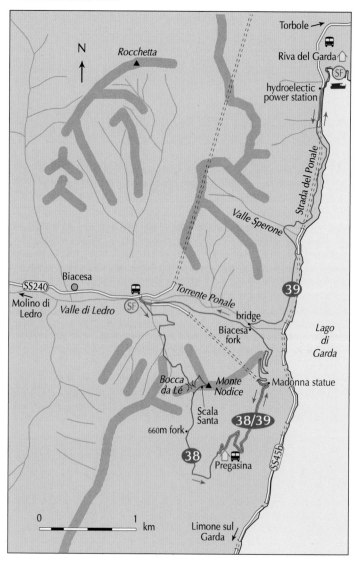

WALK 38
Monte Nodice and Pregasina

Start/Finish	Bus stop 'Bivio per Pregasina' (Pregasina turn-off) near Biacesa
Distance	8.5km (5.3 miles)
Ascent/Descent	600m/600m
Difficulty	Grade 2–3 (Grade 3 section avoidable)
Walking time	3hr 10min
Access	From Riva del Garda take the Trentino Trasporti bus for Molino di Ledro to the first stop after the road tunnel, where a minor road forks L for Pregasina.

A wonderful circuit that takes in a fascinating – albeit modest – mountain, 859m Monte Nodice. As its alternative name Cima di Lé (peak of the lake) suggests, it rises from the very edge of the lake, ensuring exciting views that reach north to embrace the Alps beyond the spectacular expanse of Lago di Garda. The path passes evidence of wartime structures then goes through the beautifully located village of Pregasina, where the cafés do a roaring trade with walkers. After a short leg of tarmac comes the old pot-holed road, reserved for walkers and cyclists these days on its crazy winding plunge to Torrente Ponale, accompanied by stunning views.

The mountain is riddled with **military structures** dating back to the pre-World War I period when the region belonged to the Austro-Hungarian Empire. These take the shape of trenches and an amazing diagonal stone staircase up a natural cleft ledge.

▶ From the bus stop turn L (E) along the surfaced road for Pregasina to the well-signed start of path n.429 (340m). Prepare for the well-graded climb through woodland on a clear path SE with plentiful red/white waymarks. The uphill pace is steady; after several lines of overgrown trenches the way steepens with loose stones underfoot, finally reaching the saddle **Bocca da Lé** (800m, 1hr

Energetic souls who make an early start can combine this route with Walk 39, part of which can also be used as a variant return route for Walk 38.

If you don't have a head for heights and prefer to avoid the dizzy stretches, from Bocca da Lé proceed straight ahead, in descent (south) to pick up the Pregasina path.

10min). Ignore the path branch R but soon keep L on an unmarked path for good lake views from military structures and a cave. ◄

Keep L then R following red dots to clamber up a rock face W, with some exposure – take special care here. It quickly leads to a wide ledge at a cavern and well-placed benches on a breathtaking belvedere platform with dizzying views down Lago di Garda and a bird's-eye view over the village of Pregasina. Now the path drops a tad, and soon there's a detour to the L along more trenches to amazing views from modest **Monte**

The Scala Santa leading down from Monte Nodice

Nodice (859m, 10min), up the top of the lake and the Sarca valley beyond Riva del Garda and Torbole. Retrace your steps to where the red dots point downwards on a narrow path for the **Scala Santa** (holy staircase!), a spectacular flight of steps cut into the rock face, equipped with a cable handrail.

It zigzags down past caverns, and veers R through a cleft in the rock and along SW to soon rejoin the main path from Bocca da Lé. Proceeding S, watch your step on the loose stones. At 660m, fork L onto path n.422, soon steep and concreted in parts. Down at a minor road, branch L to the **Chiesa di Pregasina** (532m, 40min), beautifully placed at the foot of Monte Nodice and a superb inspiring outlook across the lake. Stick to the road down past Hotel Panorama with its inviting café-terrace. Past fields and Albergo Rosalpina the surfaced way N narrows, en route to the Regina Mundi **Madonna statue** at Brion (390m, 20min).

The Regina Mundi statue below Pregasina

This superb **platform** is a great place for admiring the windsurfers and sailing boats zipping by on the lake at your feet, backed by lopsided Monte Brione.

The road soon enters a tunnel, but you fork R on the old route, now free of traffic (apart from cyclists). It zig-zags madly in descent, the surface badly eroded in parts. By all means take the 'pedonale' (pedestrian) shortcuts, though be warned that they are steep and stony. Bearing L (NNW) under a cliff, the way approaches Torrente Ponale and its valley. Keep your eyes skinned for the **Biacesa fork** L (25min), which leaves the old road to head inland (W), unless you wish to continue to Riva del Garda as follows.

Variant: Strada del Ponale return to Riva del Garda (1hr)

To carry on to Riva del Garda, stick to the old road that soon crosses a **bridge** then curves around the dramatic cliff line en route to Riva del Garda – see Walk 39.

On the opposite bank runs a historic road built in the 1840s to link the villages in the Lago di Ledro valley with Riva del Garda – see Walk 39.

The 'Sentiero del Ponale', which follows the valley inland, takes its name from the river. A lovely paved way heading W into woodland, it is hewn out of the rock here. After a shrine a milestone from 1746 is passed, evidence of the historical importance of the lane, which levels out here. ◄

The path turns R onto the modern road for Pregasina; only minutes along is the path fork for n.429, then the bus stop (45min) on the Riva–Molino road.

WALK 39

Strada del Ponale to Pregasina

Start/Finish	Riva del Garda ferry wharf
Distance	12km (7.5 miles)
Ascent/Descent	470m/470m
Difficulty	Grade 1
Walking time	4hr 15min
Access	Riva del Garda can be reached by ferry and buses from Rovereto (Trentino Trasporti), Verona (ATV) and the western shore (Brescia Trasporti).

On the northwestern shore of Lago di Garda steep limestone cliffs plunge hundreds of metres to the glittering waters below. Such geography makes for difficult access, and road builders were true pioneers, hewing lengthy stretches through mountainsides.

This walk, partly along the old Strada del Ponale, is suitable for every level of ability. A series of tunnels is traversed, well illuminated by natural daylight. A note of warning: keep young children well away from the precipitous edges. After the Ponale valley is crossed, the way is surfaced all the way to Pregasina, but is traffic-free as far as the Madonna statue. Pregasina has a couple of cafés and simple restaurants for lunch. There is a bus service from Riva del Garda but runs are few and far between – check with the Tourist Office beforehand. Allow plenty of extra time for photographs and admiring the spectacular views on this walk!

The **Strada del Ponale** was the inspiration of entrepreneur Giacomo Cis in the 1840s to link his home village on Lago di Idro with Riva; alas he died only days before he could see it open in 1851. Today's traffic uses a tunnel on the SS45b below, enabling walkers and mountain bikers to share the simply magnificent – albeit pot-holed – track.

▶ From the ferry wharf at **Riva del Garda** (65m) walk away from the town along the pavement of the SS45b,

See map for Walk 38.

aka Gardesana. You pass the historic **hydroelectric power station**, its façade bearing an imposing 1931 statue of the 'Genio delle Acque', the 'God of the Waters', so dubbed by the Italian poet Gabriele D'Annunzio. Just before the main road enters a tunnel fork R up to the start of the Strada del Ponale, and you are plunged straight into the first short **tunnel**, alive with swallows. Weaving in and out of the folds in the mountainside the lane climbs almost imperceptibly among cliffs studded with bright wildflowers, while the new road can occasionally be glimpsed below.

The second tunnel follow soon after; another features World War I military works including lookout posts peeking out of the rock face. After the fourth **tunnel** you swing briefly inland to cross the stream in Valle Sperone and

Many tunnels are encountered on the Strada del Ponale

ignore a path fork in the direction of a *via ferrata*. Further along you overlook a derelict hotel terrace high above an abandoned port. The road is surfaced but traffic-free as it enters a valley where the Torrente Ponale forms an attractive waterfall.

As the old road forks R for the Valle di Ledro, go L (sign for Pregasina) across the **bridge** (1hr). Ignore the **fork** R for Biacesa and you soon come across the first of the optional short (but steep) cuts marked 'pedonale' (pedestrian). In any case there are countless wide zig-zags that give you time to appreciate the engineering feat. Trees are gradually colonising the old road, their roots breaking up the surface and their branches shading walkers.

As you approach the modern road at a tunnel exit a path cuts up L to the huge Regina Mundi **Madonna statue** (390m, 1hr) at the magnificent lookout. Now it's 1.5km and 100m uphill on the narrow road shared with cars to the relaxed rural setting of **Pregasina** (532m, 30min). The village enjoys wonderful views to the head of the lake with the Sarca delta, not to mention lopsided Monte Brione. The Altissimo and Monte Baldo account for the eastern horizon opposite.

Return the same leisurely way to **Riva del Garda** (65m, 1hr 45min).

WALK 40
The Venetian Bastione

Start/Finish	Riva del Garda ferry wharf
Distance	4.5km (2.8 miles)
Ascent/Descent	320m/320m
Difficulty	Grade 1
Walking time	1hr 30min (+ extra 1hr 20min for Santa Barbara)
Access	Riva del Garda can be reached by ferry and buses from Rovereto (Trentino Trasporti), Verona (ATV) and the western shore (Brescia Trasporti).

The walk is a loop route, short and sweet, a pleasant way to spend an hour or so. There's also a café at the Bastione. The route can be extended uphill to the chapel at Santa Barbara, a further 325m in ascent, returning the same way. The chapel is a landmark for the town as it is lit up every evening and stands out like a beacon on the mountainside, appearing to float high over the lake. It was built in 1935 by miners working on the hydroelectric power station at Riva del Garda.

RIVA DEL GARDA

The lakeside township preserves a host of reminders of its time under the dominion of the Serenissima Republic of Venice, including a monumental town gate and the Bastione, a sturdy tower erected in the early 16th century on the lower reaches of Monte Rocchetta. Though it was deliberately razed to the ground by French troops in 1703, the council has recently seen fit to restore this photogenic structure. It occupies a fantastic position overlooking the upper lake and a stunning panorama of red-tiled roofs and clustered houses in the town's maze of medieval and Renaissance streets.

From the ferry wharf at **Riva del Garda** (65m) turn inland and cross **Piazza 3 Novembre**, passing the elegant Municipio building. On the corner with Hotel Portici turn R along Via Fiume past houses and shops. This leads

out of the pedestrian *centro storico* via the 11th-century gate **Porta San Marco**, aptly named for the patron saint of Venice.

A bird's-eye view of Riva del Garda from the Bastione

Turn L on Via Bastione and L again at the Gardacar building up to the main road SS45b, aka Gardesana. Cross over to the sign for the continuation of Via Bastione, now a surfaced lane heading uphill W. Tight zigzags lead past villas and delightful terraced gardens bursting with all manner of luxuriant vegetation. Inviting benches occupy strategic spots along the way. At a signed fork, keep L for the **Bastione** (210m, 30min). The partially restored tower doubles as a magnificent belvedere, the adjoining café an added bonus.

From the rear of the structure go up path n.404, a series of steps climbing through thick conifer

223

The Venetian Bastione

woodland. Around 15min on is a dirt forestry trail and a signed junction (350m), and the extension to Santa Barbara.

Extension to Santa Barbara (1hr 20min return)
Go L to a fork, then R for the signed climb to a hut Capanna Santa Barbara (560m) and the start of a climbing route (which you ignore). A little further along S is the tiny landmark chapel of **Santa Barbara** (625m), a superb spot. Return to the forestry trail to continue with the walk.

Go R along the **forestry trail**, a level route heading N. Where it reaches a concrete lane fork R downhill through woodland dotted with Mediterranean plants. Rather steep at times – to the joy of mountain bikers – it passes another link to the Bastione and plunges towards road level. As the first houses are encountered, branch R on a paved pedestrian-only way down to the Englovacanza B&B. Go R down to the main road (Gardesana), and R again to the Gardacar where you branch L to resume the walk back into the *centro storico* via Porta San Marco and from there to the ferry wharf at **Riva del Garda** (65m, 45min).

WALK 41

Monte Brione

Start/Finish	Riva del Garda, Piazza 3 Novembre
Distance	7.5km (4.7 miles)
Ascent/Descent	300m/300m
Difficulty	Grade 1–2
Walking time	2hr 15min
Access	Riva del Garda can be reached by ferry and buses from Rovereto (Trentino Trasporti), Verona (ATV) and the western shore (Brescia Trasporti).

Monte Brione is a curious inclined slab that rises from the otherwise flat northern edge of Lago di Garda, resembling a lopsided layered sponge cake. The western slope hosts a massive olive grove whose light-coloured foliage contrasts with the dark greens of the evergreen Mediterranean vegetation. Monte Brione was the focus of a sprawling system of defensive forts erected by the Austro-Hungarian Empire from the mid-1800s through to World War I, after which the region became the Trentino and part of Italy.

This is a lovely straightforward walk; take a picnic. The lakefront promenade is followed by a steady climb on a stepped path. Wonderful lake and alpine views accompany walkers to the string of forts.

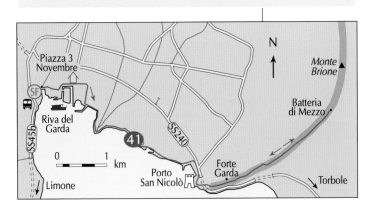

View from Monte Brione through olive trees to the Riva hinterland

At **Riva del Garda** (65m) from the lakefront **Piazza 3 Novembre** take the *lungolago* lakefront pedestrian promenade ESE. Through parks with comical duck colonies and past a modest beach, it reaches a marina and **Porto San Nicolò** (20min). At the old stone fort (1860–62) turn L up steps with a wooden handrail. This brings you to a surfaced road (Via Monte Brione) and a sign pointing R for the long-distance Sentiero della Pace (path of peace), which you follow.

A stepped path at first, it climbs steadily through holm oak and cypress trees following the edge of the crest curving NE. Concrete bunkers are passed belonging to **Forte Garda** that dates back to 1907. Well-placed benches encourage appreciation of superb views over Torbole and its tribe of windsurfers, the Sarca river and its inland fish farms, and the delta where blue-brown waters mix, and beyond to sprawling Monte Baldo. The going is breathtaking, but it gets even better with every step! At olive groves keep R on to the 1900 fortress **Batteria di Mezzo** (332m, 1hr 15min), a position that regales vast views over the Riva del Garda hinterland. ◀

Return to **Riva del Garda** (65m, 1hr) the same way.

The true top of Monte Brione is further north, and studded with antennas. The path is interrupted by fencing, though a narrow slippery route can be taken.

226

WALK 42
Torbole to Tempesta

Start	Torbole ferry wharf
Finish	Tempesta bus stop
Distance	6.3km (4 miles)
Ascent/Descent	270m/270m
Difficulty	Grade 2
Walking time	2hr 10min
Access	Torbole can be reached by ferry and buses from Riva del Garda and Rovereto (Trentino Trasporti), or Verona (ATV). The ferry wharf is on the southern edge, just south of the Tourist Office. An ATV bus covers the return stretch.

The lower northern reaches of Monte Baldo are explored on this exciting and highly panoramic walk. Courtesy of the Forestry Commission (as part of a forest fire prevention project) a *sentiero attrezzato* is followed, a clear path fitted with well-secured raised iron walkways and ladder-staircases crossing two precipitous outcrops on a wild inaccessible mountainside: almost 400 steps are negotiated in descent. There is no dangerous exposure, and handrails are present at all times. At times it feels like Corsica, with typical *maquis*-like plants and the sight of the sparkling blue 'Mediterranean Sea'!

Towards the end there is an optional return loop on a forestry track instead of descending to Tempesta and the bus back to Torbole. Check times beforehand as an hour may pass between runs.

An amazing **tale of intrigue and stealth** was played out here in the 15th century. The Venetians were losing territory to the Milanese, and craftily transported boats overland to launch them in the lake – see the Lago di Garda Introduction to read more!

From the ferry wharf at **Torbole** (56m), turn L to Hotel Ifigenia and go R on Via Pescicoltura for the 'scalinata'. The flight of steps in question is first R (E), and will see you puffing uphill. Then cross over the road and continue

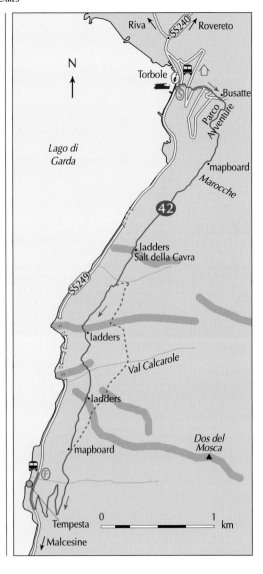

in the same direction up through a park. This ends at a road near a cliff face – keep uphill past Hotel Villa Gloria. A path soon short-cuts through the wood to a car park and lane.

Turn sharp R here to the sign 'Sentiero Panoramico Busatte–Tempesta' that leads straight through the **Busatte Parco Avventure** (201m). After a bike track layout you descend slightly to fork L on a gravel lane. Heading uphill through woodland, it curves under cliffs entering the Marocche, an ancient 'rock glacier' dotted with chaotically fallen slabs and boulders. The official start of the Busatte–Tempesta route is soon announced by a map

Walker on the sequence of steep ladders crossing wild bushland

board (40min). This also doubles as a lovely belvedere taking in the head of the lake with Riva del Garda and the neighbouring cliffs with, clearly visible, the horizontal line of the Strada del Ponale (see Walk 39).

Follow the arrow straight on to the well-kept path S, fitted with benches and information panels. The vegetation is essentially Mediterranean, dominated by holm oak and brightened with rockroses. It's not far along to the first of the exciting **ladder-staircases** (116 steps), essential to get around the aptly named outcrop **Salt della Cavra** ('goat leap'). The wonderfully scenic path then proceeds to the **second set of ladders**, even longer and more thrilling, down sheer cliffs on Corno del Bò (238 steps).

A brief uphill stretch and you're at the **third and final set of ladders** across Val Calcarole (33 steps). At a lane, a map board marking the end of the official path is soon reached (1hr), also showing a variant return.

Return variant (1hr 40min)

By branching L up the lane for an uphill section, you can loop back to rejoin the outward path between the first and second ladders. Thereafter retrace your steps via the **Busatte Parco Avventure** and back down to **Torbole**.

Turn R down the lane in wide curves with views across the lake to Limone. When you reach the roadside, turn R along the SS249 for 5min to the bus stop at **Tempesta** (36m, 30min), where there is nothing in the way of a village; for lakeside cafés return to Torbole.

WALK 43

Monte Baldo: Ventrar to San Michele

Start	Bocca Tratto Spino cable-car station
Finish	San Michele cable-car station
Distance	11.2km (7 miles)
Descent	1160m
Difficulty	Grade 2–3
Walking time	3hr (+ 30min for cable car)
Access	Malcesine is reached by ferry or ATV bus from Torbole or Torri del Benaco and Verona; the *funivia* (cable car) station is very close to the town centre. It is possible to drive to San Michele.

Beginning with a thrilling ride on the ultra-modern Malcesine *funivia* (cable car), this excellent route strikes out along the panoramic top of Monte Baldo via the Colma di Malcesine, an isolated crest with marvellous all-round views. The renowned Ventrar route, which follows, entails crossing a string of gullies with stretches that rate as Grade 3 due to occasional exposure. Afterwards (unless you opt for the shorter variant return that climbs back up to Bocca Tratto Spino), straightforward paths and lanes descend through flower-filled meadows to San Michele for the return ride to Malcesine. It is also possible to walk down to Malcesine (mostly on surfaced roads); follow signs carefully and allow 1hr 30min.

There are cafés and restaurants at Bocca Tratto Spino and Ristorio Prai Bar during the descent, but carry plenty of drinking water. Allow at least 30min for the *funivia* trip, to cover ticket purchase and queuing for the two stages. Check the timetable so you don't miss the last ride at walk's end (see Lago di Garda Introduction).

Despite its proximity to the lakeside and 'beach-holiday' atmosphere, **Monte Baldo** is alpine in both ambience and terrain. Walkers should wear boots (not trainers), and avoid bad weather as low cloud makes orientation a problem. Take warm clothing and wet-weather gear, even if you start out in warm conditions and brilliant sunshine.

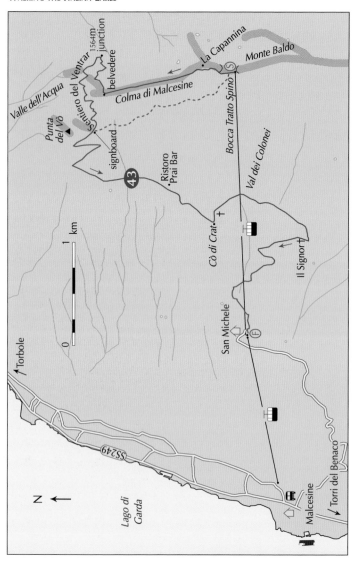

Where the cable car deposits you at the saddle **Bocca Tratto Spino** (1720m), take time to catch your breath and drink in the gorgeous vast views. The humpbacks of Monte Baldo stretch out due south, while east is the Val Brentonico. Leaving behind the cafés and restaurants, turn L (N) on the stony track for **La Capannina**, and continue along the broad grassy crest, a breathtaking walk looking north-northeast to the incline slope of Monte Altissimo. ▶ The **belvedere** extremity of the **Colma di Malcesine** (1750m, 20min) looks north to the snow-capped Adamello and Brenta groups and the spectacular top end of Lago di Garda with Riva del Garda and Torbole. A wonderful spot that is justifiably popular.

Fork R (E) on the 'Sentiero Naturalistico' down the fence line on a steep stony path, watching your step. Floral treats here come in the shape of dogroses, yellow gentians and gorgeous peonies, while in terms of fauna, marmots are guaranteed. Down at a lane and **1564m junction**, branch L for **Sentiero del Ventrar**, n.3. Not far along, you're pointed L again (W), at the head of Valle dell'Acqua. The clear path winds through woods and dwarf mountain pines, in and out of awesome gullies

Summertime here brings thick carpets of globeflowers, forget-me-nots, martagon lilies and bistort, while the air is thick with twittering skylarks and soaring eagles.

The amazing views from the belvedere

and natural ledges where rock columns stand sentinel. Several long lengths of hand cable are encountered, as are brilliant viewing points down to the lake. In 30min you're out of the gullies close to Punta del Vò, and at a signboard marking the end of Sentiero del Ventrar (1560m, 50min). A wonderful picnic spot, with the vast slope beneath the Cime del Ventrar affording magnificent views to the lake and across to Limone, not to mention Malcesine far below. The variant return route strikes out from here, as follows.

Return to Bocca Tratto Spino (45min)
From the signboard (1560m) it is feasible to take the clear if narrow path n.16 marked in red/white that cuts SSE in constant ascent across the flowered slope, concluding at **Bocca Tratto Spino** and the upper cable-car station.

From the **signboard** follow the path downhill marked for 'Prai ristorante/bar'. Amidst spreads of white St Bruno's lilies, it proceeds NW flanked by walls dating back to World War I. A sharp bend L marks the start of wide curves through lush meadows bright with orange lilies. Still as n.3 the way becomes a lane S past chalets and huts in farmland. After **Ristoro Prai Bar** (1300m, 30min) continue in gentle descent to a panoramic bench set on the outcrop **Cò di Crat** (1214m).

Now the lane takes a plunge S past a shrine down Val dei Colonei under the *funivia* cables and into woodland. Further on is the path junction **Il Signor** (981m, 30min) where you keep R through a curious chapel whose roof covers the track. It contains plaques in memory of accident victims from the 1870s. An old paved track (n.2/3) NE heads downhill through conifers and past benches, the steeper stretches of the lane cemented over. After wide curves and passing under the cables again, you reach rural landscape with farms then the tiny settlement of **San Michele** (561m, 50min) and the middle station of the cable car, not to mention the inviting café terrace of nearby Locanda Monte Baldo. This is the conclusion of the walk.

WALK 44

Monte Baldo: Cima delle Pozzette

Start/Finish	Bocca Tratto Spino cable-car station
Distance	10.5km (6.5 miles)
Ascent/Descent	415m/415m
Difficulty	Grade 2
Walking time	2hr 45min (+ 30min for cable car)
Access	Malcesine is reached by ferry or ATV bus from Torbole or Torri del Benaco and Verona; the *funivia* (cable car) station is very close to the town centre

An exquisitely panoramic walk along the crest of Monte Baldo to the Cima delle Pozzette above the northeastern shores of Lago di Garda. The day begins with the thrilling two-stage cable-car ride from Malcesine (allow at least an extra 30min for queuing, ticket purchase and the change of cabin en route).

The initial section follows the broad north–south crest of Monte Baldo, which gradually narrows as it ascends in a series of humps. This popular route is well within the capability of average walkers, though it is inadvisable prior to mid-June in case of late-lying snow which can cover waymarking and may be dangerous. Pick a clear day and start out as early as possible to beat cloud cover.

In calm conditions experienced walkers who do not suffer from vertigo can extend the route to 2218m **Cima Valdritta**, the loftiest point on Monte Baldo. This entails a further 3hr on a constantly exposed ridge (Grade 3+ – see below).

From the cable-car station at **Bocca Tratto Spino** (1720m), turn R (S) and set out downhill past the **Baita dei Forti** restaurant. At the dirt track and winter ski lift go straight up the shoulder on the other side, on well-trodden path n.651. It climbs steadily through grass and alpenrose

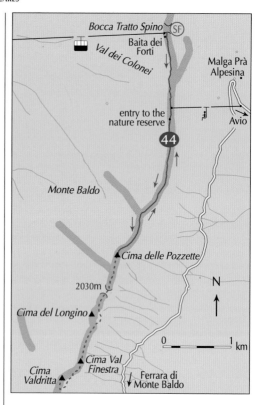

shrubs, though your attention will undoubtedly be drawn to the wonderful views of the lake and Monte Baldo peaks ahead. You reach a **chair lift** (1833m, 30min) that comes from Pra Alpesina on the eastern flanks. From here are great bird's-eye views of Malcesine on its promontory.

The path soon enters the Lastoni Selva Pezzi **Nature Reserve** where walkers must not leave the red/white marked path for any reason. You traverse meadows bright with scented daphne and primulas, heading steadily uphill with exciting glimpses of the Adige river valley to the east and the Pasubio massif beyond. The path moves gradually

The entrance to the Nature Reserve

SSW to become rockier, narrowing a little to pass through corridors of springy dwarf mountain pine, requiring the occasional hands-on scramble. With an all-round outlook you gain the wooden cross on **Cima delle Pozzette** (2132m, 1hr), a magnificent spot that feels like the top of the world! The dramatic cliffs around Campione on the western shores of Lago di Garda can be admired, along with the sweep of the lower lake and the plain.

Extension to Cima Valdritta (3hr return)

Weather and energy permitting, continue SSW in steep descent at first along the rapidly narrowing ridge route to a 2030m **saddle**. Veering L the path detours below **Cima del Longino**. Fixed cables then guide walkers along to 2086m **Cima Val Finestra** prior to Forcella di Valdritta (2107m). Here a tricky scramble detours to the peak of **Cima Valdritta** (2218m, 1hr 30min). This is the highest point on Monte Baldo. Afterwards, taking great care, retrace your steps to **Cima delle Pozzette** (1hr 30min).

In terms of panoramas, the return leg to **Bocca Tratto Spino** (1720m, 1hr 15min) is almost better than the outward climb as you are now looking north towards the Alps.

WALK 45

Monte Baldo: Eremo SS Benigno e Caro

Start	San Michele middle cable-car station
Finish	Hotel Cassone bus stop
Distance	12.5km (7.8 miles)
Ascent/Descent	570m/1050m
Difficulty	Grade 1–2
Walking time	3hr 30min (+ 20min for cable car)
Access	The *funivia* (cable-car) station at Malcesine is close to the town centre. Alight at the middle station (San Michele). From Cassone an ATV bus or the hourly summer shuttle Tourist Bus returns to Malcesine.

A long but straightforward route along the midriff of Monte Baldo high above the town of Malcesine. Very few other walkers will be encountered as you wander through farmland and dense woodland to an atmospheric chapel on the site of a remote and ancient *eremo* (hermitage) at the foot of towering cliffs in a dramatic valley. The ensuing descent to the lakeside takes steep pathways and lanes to the flourishing olive groves of Cassone, from where it's but a short bus ride back to Malcesine.

No cafés or shops are encountered en route so take lunch and drinking water.

From **San Michele** (561m) walk uphill to the signpost for path n.13 and continue up past a house to a clear junction. Ignore the fork L for Monte Baldo and go R (S) on the forestry track (n.13) to reach the **Chiesa di San Michele**. Keep following the red/white waymarks down the stony path SSW between meadows and small farms in common with a mountain bike (MTB) trail for a while. Steep at times, it drops to a house (**Le Vignole**) and a concreted road.

Where this veers R, keep straight ahead above farming settlements and olive groves in Val di Monte. Flanking a fence around a State Forest (*Foresta Demaniale*), an undulating forestry lane leads past new housing and

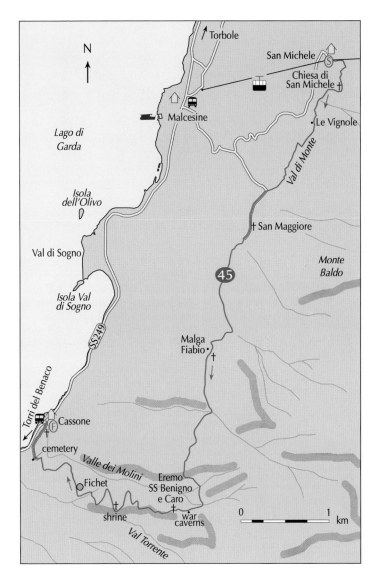

San Maggiore shrine

through to a surfaced road. You've now joined n.1; fork L uphill on the tarmac past fields and farms at the base of the awesome inclined forested slabs of Monte Baldo. A handy landmark soon reached is the roadside shrine of **San Maggiore** (435m, 45min). A gravel lane then leads past a quiet group of houses, including an *Agriturismo* with lovely lake views.

A lane leads steadily uphill through beech woodland for a long stretch, finally veering R and up to power lines and a pylon on a broad shoulder hosting the abandoned farm of **Malga Fiabio** (721m, 45min). Bright with orange lilies, the clearing gives wonderful views over the lake and up to the jagged towers and cliffs of Monte Baldo virtually overhead. Continuing S the way passes a shrine and proceeds uphill into wood. Not far along is a modest rock 'gateway'; thereafter the altitude oscillates around the 800m mark for a while. An abrupt descent takes a cutting through pink limestone with a view to magnificent cliffs opposite on the shovel-shaped Pala di San Zeno, its majesty becoming clearer as you traverse Valle dei Molini.

Mountain stream as it reaches the lake

241

Curving R (W), it's not far past **wartime rock caverns** to the **Eremo SS Benigno e Caro** (830m, 45min). The charming spot is alive with birdsong. The reconstructed church is locked, though the original cell where the hermits dwelt is always open. The building looks up to a clutch of peaks and rock points on the highest part of Monte Baldo, impossible slopes cloaked in trees.

> The cell was the long-term dwelling of two 8th-century hermits **Benigno and Caro**, renowned for their wisdom. King Pepin, son of the Holy Roman Emperor Charlemagne, came often to seek their counsel. ('SS' stands for *santi*, saints.)

Only metres along the path from the building a bench affords a lovely outlook over the lake. Soon, past trenches and crumbling walls dating back to World War I, an old paved mule track (n.1) heads downhill on a shoulder outcrop between two deep dramatic valleys that plunge directly from the summits of the Monte Baldo range. Near a **shrine** (542m) is an excellent viewpoint back up Val Torrente to Monte Telegrafo.

Continue down to the hamlet of **Fichet** (304m) where a concreted lane leads through extensive olive groves, the glittering lake visible between the trees. Down at a **cemetery** opposite playing fields, turn R via a church to the main lakeside road at **Cassone** (80m, 1hr 15min). Immediately R is the bus stop near Hotel Cassone where the mountain stream from Valle dei Molini flows towards the lake.

WALK 46
Monte Baldo: Rifugio Telegrafo Circuit

Start	Rifugio Fiori di Baldo, chair lift arrival
Finish	Rifugio Mondini, *cabinovia* arrival
Distance	13km (8 miles)
Ascent/Descent	690m/950m
Difficulty	Grade 2–3
Walking time	4hr (+ 1hr for lifts)
Access	Prada Alta (1000m) – where the first lift starts – can be reached by summer Walk&Bike bus (ATV) from Verona via San Zeno di Montagna (not daily). Cars can park at Prada Alta.

A wonderful day out on the southern slopes of Monte Baldo. The day's fun begins with a 'white-knuckle' ride in an open-sided *cabinovia* as far as Malga Prada, formerly known as Rifugio Mondini. It runs from mid-June to early October, as does the linked system, a single-seater chair lift to friendly café-restaurant Rifugio Fiori del Baldo, giving easy access for day walkers to the flower-covered slopes and high ridges of Monte Baldo. The first lift was completely rebuilt a couple of years ago and it was decided to retain the original style rather than replace it with a modern system.

This circuit (initially Grade 1) follows old wartime trails with stunning views as far as hospitable Rifugio Telegrafo. Afterwards steeper (and quieter) Grade 2 paths are followed. Clear weather is essential for both views and orientation, but low cloud and mist are common, so be warned – such conditions can make it hard to find the paths, especially on the return stretch.

From the chair lift at **Rifugio Fiori del Baldo** (1815m) turn uphill (N) on the wide stony track that passes beneath **Rifugio Chierego** and a chapel (see variant below).

Variant via Rifugio Chierego
A narrowish path from **Rifugio Fiori del Baldo** climbs via **Rifugio Chierego** then takes a rather exposed path n.658

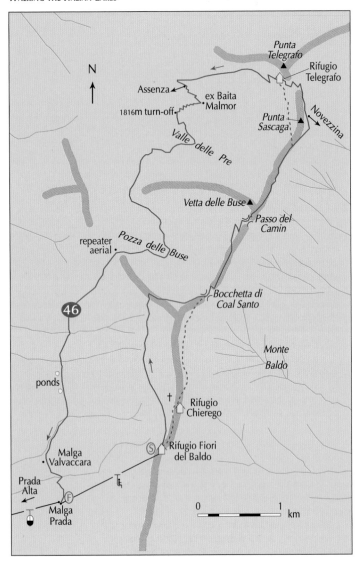

Rifugio Telegrafo

that cuts below the main ridge to **Bocchetta di Coal Santo** (1983m, 30min).

Summer walkers will take this very slowly as there are many, many wildflowers to admire and photograph, not to mention gorgeous lake views. Alpenrose shrubs take over on the higher slopes, then dwarf mountain pine as you bear R (E) over a side valley to the saddle **Bocchetta di Coal Santo** (1983m, 30min).

The way (n.658) heads NE now in gentle ascent to the rocky 'gateway' **Passo del Camin** (2126m) adjacent to Vetta delle Buse. A spectacular World War I mule track

Take the *scorciatoia* (shortcut) n.670 due north if you don't mind a little exposed scrambling.

leads in and out of weird and wonderful rock pinnacles and soon flanks the magnificent cirque Valle delle Pre, home to chamois and edelweiss. Beyond nearby **Punta Sascaga** the *rifugio* building is visible. ◄ Keep to the wide track circling R past the turn-off for Novezzina, then up for the fork L under the goods cableway over the rise to welcoming **Rifugio Telegrafo** (2142m, 1hr) beneath the eponymous mountain.

Below the building take the clear path past the chapel with red/white markings for n.654. It descends gently W, high over a cirque. After a long straight stretch, it veers L then R to a brown sign (30min) – here you leave the path headed for Assenza and instead fork L on 'Sentiero Naturalistico'. Wide zigzags lead S through dwarf mountain pine into a pasture platform once occupied by a summer farm (**ex Baita Malmor** 1884m). The path goes R for a short stretch then soon careers down a gully.

Take care not to miss the 1816m **turn-off** L (20min) – an arrow painted on the rock shows the way. Hugging a cliff base, you move into the wild neighbouring gully, the way narrow but clear. A tunnel of dwarf pines leads to a clump of fractured fallen rocks (marked by a pole for point n.8 on the Sentiero Naturalistico). Here you veer R around a white rock barrier and through a sea of conifers then up, up and steeply up to an unnamed saddle (n.7 on Sentiero Naturalistico) with dizzy views to Lago di Garda.

The path curves L (SE) to enter the superb vast cirque **Pozza delle Buse** dominated by Vette delle Buse, so named for its sinkholes. Marmots galore! In gradual descent you leave the amphitheatre W past a huge **repeater aerial**, and Prada Alta and the lake soon come into sight below. The path is fainter now, often confused with the tracks of sheep brought up here to graze in the summer months. Continue cutting S diagonally across the grassy slopes to join a lane heading in the direction of the lifts.

After a gate, pass to the L of two ponds. Immediately after the second, go over a rise then veer abruptly R in

descent touching on **Malga Valvaccara**, a stone farmhouse with a distinctive round pigeon tower. It's not far now to café-restaurant **Malga Prada** (1554m, 1hr 20min) and the lift back down to **Prada Alta** (1000m).

A misty arrival in Pozza delle Buse

> **Rifugio Telegrafo** (Tel. 045 7731797) is open from June to late September and provides dormitory beds, meals and snacks such as their trademark *Torta sbrisolona*. Summer accommodation is also available at **Rifugio Fiori del Baldo** (Tel. 045 6862477 www.fioridelbaldo. it) and **Rifugio Chierego** (Tel. 045 7732576, Mob. 348 8916235).

WALK 47

Monte Baldo: Costabella to Prada Alta

Start	Rifugio Fiori del Baldo, chair lift
Finish	Prada Alta
Distance	9.7km (6 miles)
Descent	820m
Difficulty	Grade 1–2
Walking time	2hr 40min (+ 40min for lifts)
Access	Prada Alta (1000m) – where the first lift starts – can be reached by summer Walk&Bike bus (ATV) from Verona via San Zeno di Montagna (not daily). Cars can park at Prada Alta.

A brilliantly panoramic circuit on the gentle southern-facing slopes of the Monte Baldo massif, a riot of wildflowers in early summer. The day starts with two leisurely yet exciting lift rides (see Walk 46) as far as the gorgeously panoramic Rifugio Fiori del Baldo. A broad scenic ridge is followed in gentle descent to an imposing World War I fort, and pasture clearings and beech woodland traversed on the return leg. Chances are good of finding the gorgeous vermilion wild peonies that bloom in the clearings from May to June.

Prada Alta has a café-restaurant, hotel, campsite and supermarket, and Rifugio Fiori del Baldo (www.fioridelbaldo.it) does drinks and meals.

Alight from the chair lift at **Rifugio Fiori del Baldo** (1815m) and give yourself a minute to take in the superb views over Lago di Garda, up to Monte Baldo and beyond vast pasture slopes east towards the Adige valley. Walk in front of the *rifugio* building and pick up the red/white marked path which moves off a tad above a lane. A delightful route, it meanders S along the grassy ridge, aptly named **Costabella**. A veritable carpet of wildflowers is traversed and enthusiasts will spot myriad orchids, lilies, edelweiss and scented alpine pinks, to mention but a few.

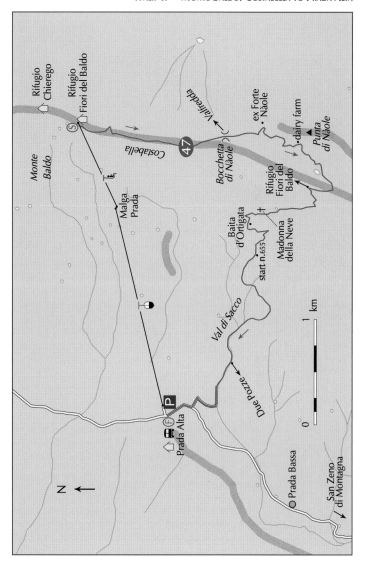

The old military lane leading from the fort

Further on is the col **Bocchetta di Nàole** (1651m, 40min) where a well-trodden path ascends from Valfredda. Here turn R but soon leave the marked path as you need to fork L through a nettle patch then a low stone wall for the gentle ascent to a path junction beneath a power line. Not far along, the path curves L to the sheltered position of the former **Forte Nàole** (1675m).

The huge rambling structure of the **fort** has been partially restructured and its top is punctuated with antennas which do not detract from its historic interest.

Continue R along an old military lane curving past a hollow with ruined buildings, and soon it's L past a summer **dairy farm** and pond. In summer the area is thick with both pasque flowers and marmots. The lane leads SW up to the main ridge once more, and sparkling Lago di Garda comes back into sight beyond woods and pasture clearings. Close at hand are thick bushes of juniper, veritable forests of yellow gentians and wine-red columbine flowers. A short stretch in descent N leads to a signed fork (R for Rifugio Fiori del Baldo) – go L for a couple of minutes and leave the lane to fork R on a path marked with stones and soon red/white waymarks. N.655 descends N through beech woodland where dog roses grow thick and colourful to a clearing with cows and the chapel of **Madonna della Neve** (1438m, 40min). The path continues close to a stone farmhouse with a characteristic dovecote tower, **Baita d'Ortigata** (1421m), aptly named for the nettles which flourish here. A lane leads downhill past stalls, in wide curves.

Gorgeous peonies abound in the woods

Keep your eyes peeled as 10min from the chapel at a bend you need to branch R (NW) on path **n.655**. This leads gently down pretty Val di Sacco through clearings and beech woods. Down at a stock gate and T-junction (where a sign points L for Due Pozze) go R on a lane lined with wild strawberries. This drops quickly and leaves the woods at houses. Follow the surfaced road downhill for a matter of minutes, and take the first turn-off R. In sight of the Prada Alta lift head down to the main road and go R for **Prada Alta** (1000m, 1hr 10min).

WALK 48
Torri del Benaco and Graffiti

Start/Finish	Torri del Benaco, Tourist Office
Distance	12km (7.4 miles)
Ascent/Descent	320m/320m
Difficulty	Grade 1–2
Walking time	2hr 50min
Access	ATV buses between Desenzano and Riva del Garda serve Torri del Benaco, as does the occasional ferry, and (significantly) the car ferry that plies the central part of Lago di Garda to Toscolano-Maderno.

This walk mostly follows lanes and stretches of tarmac, albeit quiet. The highest point, Albisano, is a charming hamlet beautifully located above the lake and promises sweeping views and a lovely lunch thanks to its cafés and restaurants.

No difficulty is involved in the walk, but extra care is needed at junctions as the signposting is a bit patchy. Superb views across Lago di Garda are enjoyed throughout. The walk starts close to the photogenic waterfront at Torri del Benaco and the Castello Scaligero museum which has several rooms featuring the prehistoric rock engravings seen on the route.

ANCIENT ROCK ENGRAVINGS

Although the graffiti or *incisioni rupestre* (rock engravings) on the thickly wooded San Vigilio promontory between Garda and Torri del Benaco are a little over-rated when compared with the magnificent display in Naquane in Valcamonica (see Lago d'Iseo Introduction), they are significant in that they are ancient and testify to a long history of human presence on the eastern shore of Lago di Garda. It is thought that the artists were itinerant herders or hunters. Two sets of engravings discovered in 1964 are visited during this pleasant walk, both of which were scratched and tapped into a natural drawing board, rock slabs polished smooth by the passage of an ancient glacier.

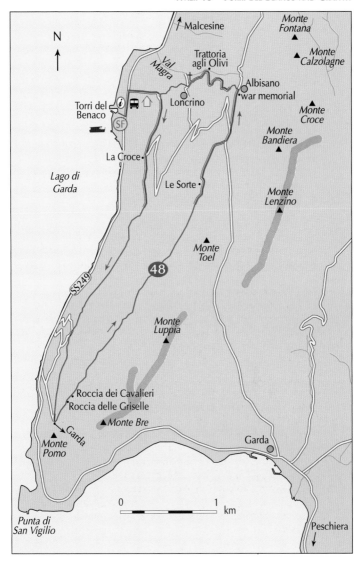

N

↑ Malcesine

Monte
Fontana ▲

Monte
Calzolagne ▲

Val
Magra

Trattoria
agli Olivi
✝

Albisano
war memorial ●

Monte
Croce ▲

Torri del
Benaco
ⓢⒻ

Loncrino ●

Monte
Bandiera ▲

La Croce ●

Lago di
Garda

Le Sorte ●

Monte
Lenzino ▲

SS249

Monte
Toel ▲

48

Monte
Luppia ▲

Roccia dei Cavalieri ●
Roccia delle Griselle ●

Garda

▲ Monte Bre

Garda ●

Monte
Pomo ▲

0   1

km

Punta di
San Vigilio

Peschiera

From the Tourist Office at **Torri del Benaco** (68m) walk away from the lake on pedestrian-only Via Fratelli Lavanda. At the main road turn L past the bus stop to the traffic lights. Now go R (E) on Via per Albisano, and continue past B&B Onda Garni. As the road curves R bounded by high stone walls, take the minor parallel road to its L. They soon join again to go uphill through a residential area, quickly reaching a curve at **La Croce**. Branch R here on Via Bellini, signed with red waymarks and n.2 for 'Graffiti'. The narrow road soon becomes a dirt lane coasting S through picturesque olive groves with great views down to the lake and Torri del Benaco and across the water to Salò and Toscolano-Maderno.

Further along the lane descends a little, and a short surfaced stretch passes houses before resuming its marvellous scenic stroll. At a second batch of houses, as the road veers R in descent, at an electricity substation fork L uphill on the signed path. This soon reaches a junction

Torri del Benaco and its castle stand out against the lake

on Monte Pomo where it is joined by the green n.3 route from Garda. A fork L on a rocky path through woods thick with smoke bushes soon leads to the first group of rock engravings beneath Monte Bre.

The lane leads through olive groves

> The glacially polished slab is referred to as **Roccia delle Griselle**, for the 'rope ladders' (*griselle*) on the ships depicted. A little further on is the **Roccia dei Cavalieri** with a line-up of 12 stick figures or 'knights' (*cavalieri*) (1hr 20min).

Keep uphill (NE) on the clear path lined with butchers' broom, ivy and holm oak, to where it widens to a lane. Ignore turn-offs and continue in the same direction past rural properties in gentle ascent underneath Monte Luppia. The way levels out and is surfaced as it passes through olive plantations and the hamlet of **Le Sorte** overlooking the lake and Torri del Benaco. A short stretch in

255

The Rocca dei Cavalieri engravings

descent brings you to the main road Via Volpara, where you go L.

Keep R at the next fork to nearby pretty **Albisano** (311m, 50min) for cafés (and even a bus back to Torri del Benaco). However just before you enter the actual square, at a pyramidal war memorial and large car park, cross the road to fork L down a flight of steps (sign for Torri).

Down at a lane, go L on a quiet tarmac road past more olive groves and houses. Then it's R at the next branch, down into pretty Val Magra and the **Trattoria agli Olivi** where you go L. Further on you pass an ancient shrine at **Loncrino**, and soon afterwards turn R down a delightful cobbled lane. This brings you out at the road Via per Albisano that leads down past Onda Garni to the traffic lights where you go L back to the Tourist Office at **Torri del Benaco** (68m, 40min).

APPENDIX A

Route summary table

Walk	Name	Time	Distance	Ascent/Descent	Grade
1	Stresa to Belgirate	2hr 30min	9km (5.6 miles)	300m/270m	1–2
2	From the Mottarone to Baveno	3hr 45min	15km (9.3 miles)	0m/1300m	2+
3	Monte Orfano and Lago di Mergozzo	4hr	13km (8 miles)	600m/600m	2–3
4	Cavandone on Monterosso	2hr 30min	8.5km (5.3 miles)	265m/265m	1–2
5	Ghiffa Sanctuary Loop	3hr	10.5km (6.5 miles)	565m/565m	1–2
6	Villages above Cannero	4hr	16.5km (10.3 miles)	800m/800m	2
7	The Cannero–Cannobio Traverse	2hr 20min	8.5km (5.3 miles)	420m/420m	1–2
8	Monte Carza	5hr	17km (10.6 miles)	900m/900m	2–3
9	Val Cannobina	5hr	20km (12.4 miles)	700m/1150m	2
10	Cannobio–San Bartolomeo in Montibus Circuit	3hr 40min	12km (7.5 miles)	450m/450m	2
11	Monteviasco	4hr	15.6km (9.7 miles)	800m/800m	1–2
12	Sasso del Ferro	2hr	8.5km (5.3 miles)	110m/850m	2
13	Colonno to Cadenabbia on the Greenway	3hr 15min	10.5km (6.5 miles)	100m/100m	1
14	San Martino Circuit	3hr	5.7km (3.5 miles)	250m/250m	1–2
15	The Bocchetta di Nava Traverse	3hr 15min	9km (5.6 miles)	500m/685m	2
16	Crocetta	1hr	3.5km (2.2 miles)	110m/110m	1

Walk	Name	Time	Distance	Ascent/Descent	Grade
17	Val Sanagra	5hr 20min	14km (8.7 miles)	550m/550m	2
18	Rifugio Menaggio and Monte Grona	4hr 40min	9km (5.6 miles)	950m/950m	2+
19	San Domenico and the Santuario di Breglia	1hr 15min	3km (1.8 miles)	60m/60m	1
20	Gravedona to Domaso	1hr 30min	4km (2.5 miles)	200m/200m	1–2
21	Domaso to Gera Lario	2hr 20min	7.5km (4.6 miles)	280m/280m	2
22	Sentiero del Viandante 1: Varenna to Bellano	2hr 45min	6.2km (3.8 miles)	270m/265m	2
23	Sentiero del Viandante 2: Bellano to Dervio	2hr 45min	6.2km (3.8 miles)	170m/135m	2
24	Around Bellagio	2hr	6km (3.7 miles)	85m/85m	1
25	Belvedere del Monte Nuvolone	4hr 15min	14km (8.7 miles)	1130m/240m	2
26	Monte San Primo	3hr 20min	7.5km (4.6 miles)	580m/580m	2+
27	The Strada Regia from Pognana Lario to Torno	3hr 30min	10.5km (6.5 miles)	360m/360m	1–2
28	Brunate to Torno Path	3hr 45min	12.5km (7.7 miles)	250m/725m	2
29	Monte Boletto	4hr 10min	10.5km (6.5 miles)	550m/550m	2
30	Punta Alta	4hr 30min	10km (6.2 miles)	850m/850m	2+
31	Santuario di San Giovanni	2hr 15min	6.5km (4 miles)	450m/450m	1–2
32	Corna Trentapassi	3hr 30min	11km (6.8 miles)	680m/680m	2–3
33	Monteisola and the Santuario della Ceriola	2hr 30min	7.5km (4.6 miles)	420m/420m	1–2
34	Eremo di San Valentino	3hr 45min	10km (6.2 miles)	650m/650m	2

Walk	Name	Time	Distance	Ascent/Descent	Grade
35	Campione to Pregasio Loop	4hr	9.7km (6 miles)	670m/670m	2
36	Limone sul Garda and the Valle del Singol	4hr 30min	10km (6.2 miles)	880m/880m	3
37	Sentiero del Sole	3hr	6.5km (4 miles)	180m/180m	1–2
38	Monte Nodice and Pregasina	3hr 10min	8.5km (5.3 miles)	600m/600m	2–3
39	Strada del Ponale to Pregasina	4hr 15min	12km (7.5 miles)	470m/470m	1
40	The Venetian Bastione	1hr 30min	4.5km (2.8 miles)	320m/320m	1
41	Monte Brione	2hr 15min	7.5km (4.7 miles)	300m/300m	1–2
42	Torbole to Tempesta	2hr 10min	6.3km (4 miles)	270m/270m	2
43	Monte Baldo: Ventrar to San Michele	3hr	11.2km (7 miles)	0m/1160m	2–3
44	Monte Baldo: Cima delle Pozzette	2hr 45min	10.5km (6.5 miles)	415m/415m	2
45	Monte Baldo: Eremo SS Benigno e Caro	3hr 30min	12.5km (7.8 miles)	570m/1050m	1–2
46	Monte Baldo: Rifugio Telegrafo Circuit	4hr	13km (8 miles)	690m/950m	2–3
47	Monte Baldo: Costabella to Prada Alta	2hr 40min	9.7km (6 miles)	0m/820m	1–2
48	Torri del Benaco and Graffiti	2hr 50min	12km (7.4 miles)	320m/320m	1–2

The Greenway passes Villa Balbiano (Walk 13)

APPENDIX B
Glossary of Italian–English terms

acqua (non) potabile	(un)drinkable water
affittacamere	B&B
aiuto!	help!
albergo	hotel
alimentari	grocery shop
aperto/chiuso	open/closed
aria di sosta	picnic area
attracco, imbarcadero, pontile, scalo	ferry pier, wharf, landing stage
autostazione	bus station
baita	mountain hut, often a rustic restaurant
battello	passenger ferry
bivio	junction
bocca, bocchetta	saddle, pass (lit. mouth, little mouth)
bosco	wood
caduta massi/sassi	rockfalls
calchera	lime kiln
cappella	shrine, chapel
carta escursionistica	walking map
castello	castle
centro storico	historic town centre
chiesa	church
cima	peak
cimitero	cemetery
Comune, Municipio	Town Hall
corriere, autobus	bus
costone, cresta, crinale, dorsale	crest, ridge
croce	cross
destra/sinistra	right/left
deviazione	detour
difficile/facile	difficult/easy
eremo	hermitage
faro	lighthouse
fermata dell'autobus	bus stop
fiume	river
foce	estuary
forno	oven, furnace
frana	landslide
funicolare	funicular lift
funivia	cable car
galleria	tunnel
gradinata	flight of steps
guado	stream or river ford
incisione rupestre	rock engraving
inferiore/superiore	lower/upper
isola	island
lago	lake
lungolago	lakefront promenade
maneggio	horse riding
molino, mulino	mill
montagna, monte, monti	mountain or high-altitude pasture
mulattiera	old mule track
orario	timetable
orrido	ravine
panificio	bakery
passeggiata pedonale	pedestrian promenade
pasticceria	cake shop
pedoni	pedestrians
pericolo!	danger!
piazza	village or town square
pizzo, vetta	peak
ponte	bridge
previsioni del tempo	weather forecast
pronto soccorso	first aid/emergency ward
rifugio	mountain hut
rio, torrente	mountain stream
ristoro	refreshments, café
scalinata	flight of steps
scorciatoia	shortcut
seggiovia	chair lift
sentiero	path
soccorso alpino	mountain rescue
sorgente	spring (water)
sottopassaggio	underpass
spiaggia	beach
stazione ferroviaria	railway station
sterrata	lane, unsurfaced road
strada, via	road
supermercato	supermarket
teleferica	goods cableway
torre	tower
traghetto	car ferry
trattoria	rustic-style restaurant
vecchio, vecchia	old

NOTES

NOTES

NOTES

NOTES

NOTES

LISTING OF CICERONE GUIDES